TEACHER'S PET PUBLICATIONS

LITPLAN TEACHER PACK
for
The Summer of My German Soldier

based on the book by
Bette Greene

Written by
Mary B. Collins

© 1996 Teacher's Pet Publications
All Rights Reserved

This **LitPlan** for Bette Greene's
Summer of My German Soldier
has been brought to you by Teacher's Pet Publications, Inc.

Copyright Teacher's Pet Publications 1996
11504 Hammock Point
Berlin MD 21811

Only the student materials in this unit plan
such as worksheets, study questions, assignment sheets, and tests
may be reproduced multiple times for use in the purchaser's classroom.

For any additional copyright questions,
contact Teacher's Pet Publications.

www.tpet.com

TABLE OF CONTENTS - *Summer of My German Soldier*

Introduction	5
Unit Objectives	8
Reading Assignment Sheet	9
Unit Outline	10
Study Questions (Short Answer)	13
Quiz/Study Questions (Multiple Choice)	24
Pre-reading Vocabulary Worksheets	43
Lesson One (Introductory Lesson)	55
Nonfiction Assignment Sheet	57
Oral Reading Evaluation Form	59
Writing Assignment 1	61
Writing Assignment 2	64
Writing Assignment 3	77
Writing Evaluation Form	78
Vocabulary Review Activities	72
Extra Writing Assignments/Discussion ?s	66
Unit Review Activities	79
Unit Tests	83
Unit Resource Materials	119
Vocabulary Resource Materials	133

A FEW NOTES ABOUT THE AUTHOR
Bette Greene

GREENE, BETTE (1934-   ) Like Patty Bergen, the heroine of *Summer of My German Soldier*, Bette Greene grew up in Arkansas as the daughter of a sundries store owner during World War II. She has called herself a "bad student and an even worse speller." But that didn't stop her from becoming a first-rate novelist. She has attended many colleges to further her own education, including Columbia University, Harvard, Alliance Francaise in Paris, the University of Alabama, and Memphis State University.

Summer of My German Soldier was Bette Greene's first novel, published in 1973. It was followed by *Philip Hall Likes Me, I Reckon Maybe* in 1974, *Morning is a Long Time Coming* in 1978, *Get On Out of Here, Philip Hall* in 1981, and *Them That Glitter and Them That Don't* in 1983.

She resides in Brookline, Massachusetts with her husband and two children.

INTRODUCTION

This unit has been designed to develop students' reading, writing, thinking, and language skills through exercises and activities related to *Summer of My German Soldier* by Bette Greene. It includes eighteen lessons, supported by extra resource materials.

The **introductory lesson** checks students' knowledge of some background to the novel through a bulletin board activity. Following the introductory activity, students are given a transition to explain how the activity relates to the book they are about to read. Following the transition, students are given the materials they will be using during the unit. At the end of the lesson, students begin the pre-reading work for the first reading assignment.

The **reading assignments** are approximately thirty pages each; some are a little shorter while others are a little longer. Students have approximately 15 minutes of pre-reading work to do prior to each reading assignment. This pre-reading work involves reviewing the study questions for the assignment and doing some vocabulary work for 8 to 10 vocabulary words they will encounter in their reading.

The **study guide questions** are fact-based questions; students can find the answers to these questions right in the text. These questions come in two formats: short answer or multiple choice. The best use of these materials is probably to use the short answer version of the questions as study guides for students (since answers will be more complete), and to use the multiple choice version for occasional quizzes. If your school has the appropriate machinery, it might be a good idea to make transparencies of your answer keys for the overhead projector.

The **vocabulary work** is intended to enrich students' vocabularies as well as to aid in the students' understanding of the book. Prior to each reading assignment, students will complete a two-part worksheet for approximately 8 to 10 vocabulary words in the upcoming reading assignment. Part I focuses on students' use of general knowledge and contextual clues by giving the sentence in which the word appears in the text. Students are then to write down what they think the words mean based on the words' usage. Part II nails down the definitions of the words by giving students dictionary definitions of the words and having students match the words to the correct definitions based on the words' contextual usage. Students should then have an understanding of the words when they meet them in the text.

After each reading assignment, students will go back and formulate answers for the study guide questions. Discussion of these questions serves as a **review** of the most important events and ideas presented in the reading assignments.

After students complete reading the work, there is a **vocabulary review** lesson which pulls together all of the fragmented vocabulary lists for the reading assignments and gives students a review of all of the words they have studied.

A lesson is devoted to the **extra discussion questions/writing assignments**. These questions focus on interpretation, critical analysis and personal response, employing a variety of thinking skills and adding to the students' understanding of the novel.

There is a **group activity** in which students work in small groups to explore many career opportunities related to the novel.

The group activity is followed by a **reports and discussion** session in which the groups share their information about the careers with the entire class; thus, the entire class is exposed to information about all of the careers and the entire class can discuss each career based on the nucleus of information brought forth by each of the groups.

There are three **writing assignments** in this unit, each with the purpose of informing, persuading, or having students express personal opinions. The first assignment is to express personal opinions: students write a composition in which they tell about some memorable event that has happened to them in their own lives. The second assignment is to inform: students look at the vocabulary words Patty uses near the end of chapter 7 and explain how each of those words relates to the story. The third assignment is to persuade: students choose to either prosecute or defend Patty at her trial and write a composition which would be their opening or closing remarks to the jury.

In addition, there is a **nonfiction reading assignment**. Students are required to read a piece of nonfiction related in some way to *Summer of My German Soldier*. After reading their nonfiction pieces, students will fill out a worksheet on which they answer questions regarding facts, interpretation, criticism, and personal opinions. During one class period, students make **oral presentations** about the nonfiction pieces they have read. This not only exposes all students to a wealth of information, it also gives students the opportunity to practice **public speaking**.

The **review lesson** pulls together all of the aspects of the unit. The teacher is given four or five choices of activities or games to use which all serve the same basic function of reviewing all of the information presented in the unit.

The **unit test** comes in two formats: multiple choice or short answer. As a convenience, two different tests for each format have been included. There is also an advanced short answer test for students who need more of a challenge.

There are additional **support materials** included with this unit. The **extra activities** section includes suggestions for an in-class library, crossword and word search puzzles related to the novel, and extra vocabulary worksheets. There is a list of **bulletin board ideas** which gives the teacher suggestions for bulletin boards to go along with this unit. In addition, there is a list of **extra class activities** the teacher could choose from to enhance the unit or as a substitution for an exercise the teacher might feel is inappropriate for his/her class. **Answer keys** are located directly after the **reproducible student materials** throughout the unit. The student materials may be reproduced for use in the teacher's classroom without infringement of copyrights. No other portion of this unit may be reproduced without the written consent of Teacher's Pet Publications, Inc.

UNIT OBJECTIVES - *Summer of My German Soldier*

1. To expose students to a different era of American life.

2. Students will demonstrate their understanding of the text on four levels: factual, interpretive, critical, and personal.

3. Students will discuss prejudice, aspects of family life, and relationships.

4. Students will be given the opportunity to practice reading aloud and silently to improve their skills in each area.

5. Students will answer questions to demonstrate their knowledge and understanding of the main events and characters in *Summer of My German Soldier* as they relate to the author's theme development.

6. Students will enrich their vocabularies and improve their understanding of the novel through the vocabulary lessons prepared for use in conjunction with the novel.

7. The writing assignments in this unit are geared to several purposes:
    a. To have students demonstrate their abilities to inform, to persuade, or to express their own personal ideas
        Note: Students will demonstrate ability to write effectively to <u>inform</u> by developing and organizing facts to convey information. Students will demonstrate the ability to write effectively to <u>persuade</u> by selecting and organizing relevant information, establishing an argumentative purpose, and by designing an appropriate strategy for an identified audience. Students will demonstrate the ability to write effectively to <u>express personal ideas</u> by selecting a form and its appropriate elements.
    b. To check the students' reading comprehension
    c. To make students think about the ideas presented by the novel
    d. To encourage logical thinking
    e. To provide an opportunity to practice good grammar and improve students' use of the English language.

8. Students will read aloud, report, and participate in large and small group discussions to improve their public speaking and personal interaction skills.

READING ASSIGNMENT SHEET - *Summer of My German Soldier*

Date Assigned	Chapters Assigned	Completion Date
	1-2	
	3-5	
	6	
	7-9	
	10-12	
	13-16	
	17-18	
	19-21	

UNIT OUTLINE - *Summer of My German Soldier*

1	2	3	4	5
Introduction PV 1-2	Read 1-2 PVR 3-5	Study ?s 1-5 PVR 6 PV 7-9	Read 7-9	Study ?s 6-9 Writing Assignment #1
6	7	8	9	10
PVR 10-12	Study ?s 10-12 PVR 13-16	Study ?s 13-16 Writing Assignment #2 PVR 17-18	Study ?s 17-18 PVR 19-21	Study ?s 19-21 Extra Questions
11	12	13	14	15
Quotes	Vocabulary	Group Activity	Reports & Discussion	Writing Assignment #3
16	17	18		
Nonfiction Reports	Review	**Test**		

Key: P=Preview Study Questions V=Prereading Vocabulary Worksheet R=Read

STUDY GUIDE QUESTIONS

SHORT ANSWER STUDY GUIDE QUESTIONS - *Summer of My German Soldier*

Chapters 1-2
1. Why were the Nazis coming to Jenkinsville?
2. Why was Patty disappointed upon seeing the Nazis?
3. What is a Victory Garden?
4. Who is Ruth?
5. Who is Robert?
6. Who is Sharon?
7. What was Patty's lie?
8. What does Patty's father hate about taking favors?
9. Why was it okay for Sharon to take money from Grandma?
10. How does Patty tell how grown up Grandma thinks she is?
11. What did Grandma say was the difference between Pearl and her brothers?
12. How does Patty feel when she leaves Memphis?

Chapters 3-5
1. Why did the P.O.W.s come to the Bergens' store?
2. What was different about Reiker?
3. What did Anton buy at the Bergens' store?
4. What was Patty's lie to Sister Parker?
5. Who was Edna Louise?
6. How did Patty try to punish Edna Louise? Why? Did it work?
7. What is Patty's only admitted ambition?
8. Who does Sharon look like?
9. What did Patty and Freddy play, and what was the result of their game?
10. What is different about the way Ruth sings?
11. How did Patty's father react to the broken car window?

Chapters 6-9
1. Why is Saturday Patty's favorite day of the week?
2. Why does Patty not want to go to Mrs. Reeves' place?
3. What was the reason Patty gave Mrs. Reeves for not going to Baptist training camp?
4. What is Patty's opinion of Sharon?
5. What did Patty do to the "hide out"?
6. What did Ruth do to Patty's hair?
7. Who did Patty see running to the train?
8. How did Anton react to Patty's saying his name?
9. How did Anton escape from the P.O.W. camp?
10. How did Anton react when he found out that Patty was Jewish?

Summer of My German Soldier Short Answer Study Guide Page 2

11. Who was the P.O.W. escapee about whom the townspeople were talking?
12. What did Mr. Blakey think was working in the United States?
13. What were the F.B.I. agents doing in the Bergens' store?
14. What did Patty tell the F.B.I. agent was most unusual about Reiker?
15. Who was Charlene Madlee?

Chapters 10-12
1. What was Mr. Bergen's reaction to Patty's shirt gift? Anton's reaction to the same gift?
2. Why did Patty's father beat her again, and what was Anton's reaction?
3. Why was Mrs. Bergen angry at Ruth?
4. What did Patty tell her parents about the missing food?
5. What did Ruth want Patty to tell her?
6. What did Anton reveal to Patty about her father?
7. To whom did Anton compare Mr. Bergen?
8. How did Patty expect Ruth to act when Anton offered her a chair? Did she?
9. What did Mr. Eugene Jackson do to Ruth's mother?
10. How are leaders like department stores, according to Anton?

Chapters 13-16
1. Why was Ruth worried?
2. What was Patty's plan?
3. What was Anton's last "lesson" for Patty?
4. What did Anton give to Patty?
5. Where did Harry think Sharon could go?
6. Where did Patty tell Sister Parker she got the ring?
7. Why did Harry beat Patty at the store?
8. Who came to the store to talk to Patty?
9. Why did Patty embellish her story about the tramp by telling the sheriff that the tramp had said, "I could go through this world proud and happy if only God had seen it fit to give me a daughter exactly like you"?
10. What was Patty's one gain?
11. What was Patty's loss?
12. What evidence did the F.B.I. man produce to link the Bergens to Anton?
13. What happened to Anton?

Summer of My German Soldier Short Answer Study Guide Page 3

Chapters 17-18
1. What was the reason Patty gave her father for helping Anton?
2. What happened to Ruth?
3. What did the townspeople do to Patty?
4. Why did Harry need a new job?
5. What did Pearl expect her father to do?
6. Where did Patty stay after her aid to Anton was exposed?
7. Who came to visit Patty at her grandparents' house?

Chapters 19-21
1. Why did Mr. Grimes stop off to get food for Patty and himself?
2. Why couldn't Patty mention that Mr. Grimes had taken her out to eat?
3. What was Patty's sentence?
4. What was Mr. Hollis' advice to anyone who has to go to court?
5. To what did Patty compare the screening on the windows?
6. Who is Patty's roommate?
7. What does Mavis call Patty?
8. Why is Mavis in the reformatory?
9. What set Patty apart from the rest of the girls at the reformatory?
10. Who came to visit Patty at the reformatory?
11. Who is Ruth's new boss?
12. Who does Ruth say she loves the most?
13. What did Ruth call Patty's parents?
14. What is a "nom de plume"?
15. What is Patty's pen name?
16. What did Miss Laud call Patty?
17. To what did Patty compare Ruth's leaving?
18. What did Patty learn about herself?

ANSWER KEY: SHORT ANSWER STUDY GUIDE QUESTIONS
Summer of My German Soldier

<u>Chapters 1-2</u>

1. Why were the Nazis coming to Jenkinsville?
    They were coming to the P.O.W. camp located in Jenkinsville.

2. Why was Patty disappointed upon seeing the Nazis?
    In the movies P.O.W.s look dramatic and angry. The P.O.W.s in Jenkinsville could have been a crew from the Arkansas Public Works Department. Patty was disappointed in their ordinary appearance.

3. What is a Victory Garden?
    A Victory Garden is a garden of vegetables which everyone was supposed to grow until the war was over.

4. Who is Ruth?
    Ruth is the housekeeper for Patty's family.

5. Who is Robert?
    Robert is Ruth's son who was sent off to war.

6. Who is Sharon?
    Sharon is Patty's sister who is almost six years old and is definitely the parents' favorite daughter.

7. What was Patty's lie?
    Her lie was that a P.O.W. had tried to escape and the guard tried to stop him.

8. What does Patty's father hate about taking favors?
    He hates to feel obligated to anyone.

9. Why was it okay for Sharon to take money from Grandma?
    It was okay for Sharon to take money from Grandma because Sharon was "little."

10. How does Patty tell how grown up Grandma thinks she is?
    The more grown up she is, the more wine she gets in her glass.

11. What did Grandma say was the difference between Pearl and her brothers?
    The boys always liked what they were given, but Pearl never liked anything once it was hers.

12. How does Patty feel when she leaves Memphis?
    She feels like she has just left home and is going to the place where she lives.

<u>Chapters 3-5</u>
1. Why did the P.O.W.s come to the Bergens' store?
    They came to buy straw field hats.

2. What was different about Reiker?
    He spoke English very well.

3. What did Anton buy at the Bergens' store?
    He bought a pocket pencil sharpener and a gaudy pin.

4. What was Patty's lie to Sister Parker?
    She said that Anton hated Hitler more than anyone in the world and that he prayed every night that the Americans would win the war.

5. Who was Edna Louise?
    She was a "friend" Patty went to visit. She dressed perfectly and was described as "boy-crazy." Edna Louise was the daughter of the richest man in town.

6. How did Patty try to punish Edna Louise? Why? Did it work?
    Patty was insulted by Edna Louise's comments about Reiker, so she decided to punish Edna Louise by leaving her house. No, it didn't work; Edna Louise just unemotionally told Patty goodbye.

7. What is Patty's only admitted ambition?
    She works at learning the meaning of every single word in the dictionary.

8. Who does Sharon look like?
    She looks like her mother.

9. What did Patty and Freddy play, and what was the result of their game?
    They played "hit the hubcap." As a result of their game, a stone broke the window of a passing car.

10. What is different about the way Ruth sings?
    Patty thinks she doesn't sing from her throat like most people. "Her songs always come from a deeper, quieter place than that."

11. How did Patty's father react to the broken car window?
    He beat her.

Chapters 6-9

1. Why is Saturday Patty's favorite day of the week?
    She can usually help at the store on Saturday, and she likes to do that.

2. Why does Patty not want to go to Mrs. Reeves' place?
    Mrs. Reeves is a hairdresser who apparently gives everyone the same curly-cue permanent hair style. Patty hates her hair to be all curled and frizzed-up. Also, if she goes to get her hair done, she will have to leave the store.

3. What was the reason Patty gave Mrs. Reeves for not going to Baptist training camp?
    She said that there were too many mosquitoes and black moccasin snakes there. (The real reason was, of course, that her mother did not want her to go because she was Jewish.)

4. What is Patty's opinion of Sharon?
    "Sometimes I think she's the wisest of us all. She isn't tactless like our mother or nervous like our father and she certainly doesn't always rush into trouble like me."

5. What did Patty do to the "hide out"?
    She cleaned it from top to bottom.

6. What did Ruth do to Patty's hair?
    She gave Patty a haircut and made her hair look better.

7. Who did Patty see running to the train?
    She saw Anton Reiker.

8. How did Anton react to Patty's saying his name?
    He became angry because people (the authorities) might have heard her say it.

9. How did Anton escape from the P.O.W. camp?
    He gave one of the guards (fake) diamonds (from the pin he bought at the store) in exchange for the guard's driving him out of the camp.

10. How did Anton react when he found out that Patty was Jewish?
    He was terribly surprised and then he laughed at the irony of it.

11. Who was the P.O.W. escapee about whom the townspeople were talking?
    They were talking about Anton.

12. What did Mr. Blakey think was working in the United States?
    He thought that the Nazi Underground movement was working in the U.S.

13. What were the F.B.I. agents doing in the Bergens' store?
>   They were investigating the escape of the prisoner from the P.O.W. camp. They came to the store for information. Since the escapee had once been in the store, they thought that the people there might have some clues for them.

14. What did Patty tell the F.B.I. agent was most unusual about Reiker?
>   She noted his unusual politeness.

15. Who was Charlene Madlee?
>   She was a reporter from the Memphis *Commercial Appeal* who had come to investigate the P.O.W. story.

<u>Chapters 10-12</u>

1. What was Mr. Bergen's reaction to Patty's shirt gift? Anton's reaction to the same gift?
>   Mr. Bergen said, "Thanks" and tossed the shirt aside. Anton looked at it, felt it, and showed pleasure in receiving the shirt.

2. Why did Patty's father beat her again, and what was Anton's reaction?
>   Mr. Bergen beat Patty again because he caught her talking with Freddy Dowd. When Anton saw him beating her, he ran from his hiding place and was about to defend Patty, but he realized that keeping cover was more important at that time, so he retreated.

3. Why was Mrs. Bergen angry at Ruth?
>   She thought Ruth was stealing food from the kitchen.

4. What did Patty tell her parents about the missing food?
>   She said that she had eaten the salami and that Sharon and Sue Ellen had eaten the chicken.

5. What did Ruth want Patty to tell her?
>   She wanted to know about the man who was in the garage. (Ruth had seen him come out when Mr. Bergen was beating Patty.)

6. What did Anton reveal to Patty about her father?
>   He said that after Mr. Bergen had beaten Patty, he had come to the side of the garage and said, "Nobody loves me. In my whole entire life, nobody has loved me."

7. To whom did Anton compare Mr. Bergen?
>   Anton compared Mr. Bergen to Hitler. "Cruelty is after all cruelty, and the difference between the two men may have more to do with their degrees of power than their degrees of cruelty."

8. How did Patty expect Ruth to act when Anton offered her a chair? Did she?
>Patty expected her to act embarrassed, but she did not.

9. What did Mr. Eugene Jackson do to Ruth's mother?
>He stole the money she had put away for Ruth's education.

10. How are leaders like department stores, according to Anton?
>They are both in business to "give people what they think they want."

Chapters 13-16

1. Why was Ruth worried?
>She was worried that Patty would visit Anton and that the authorities would catch the two together.

2. What was Patty's plan?
>She planned to go with Anton.

3. What was Anton's last "lesson" for Patty?
>He told her, ". . . you are a person of value, and you have a friend who loved you enough to give you his most valuable possession."

4. What did Anton give to Patty?
>He gave her a gold ring which had been in his family for generations.

5. Where did Harry think Sharon could go?
>He thought she could be successful in Hollywood.

6. Where did Patty tell Sister Parker she got the ring?
>She said she had fed a tramp and that he had given her the ring out of gratitude.

7. Why did Harry beat Patty at the store?
>He found out about the ring and did not believe that Patty had only fed the tramp. Mr. Bergen thought the tramp had given Patty the ring in exchange for letting him touch her.

8. Who came to the store to talk to Patty?
>Mr. Bergen called Sheriff Cauldwell, who came to question Patty further about the ring.

9. Why did Patty embellish her story about the tramp by telling the sheriff that the tramp had said, "I could go through this world proud and happy if only God had seen it fit to give me a daughter exactly like you"?
>Patty wanted to make her father feel bad for thinking she was a terrible daughter.

10. What was Patty's one gain?
   Her gain was that her father respected her.

11. What was Patty's loss?
   She had lost Anton.

12. What evidence did the F.B.I. man produce to link the Bergens to Anton?
   He showed Patty the shirt with her father's initials, the shirt she had given Anton.

13. What happened to Anton?
   In New York he was shot and killed while trying to escape.

Chapters 17-18
1. What was the reason Patty gave her father for helping Anton?
   She said she helped him because he was kind to her.

2. What happened to Ruth?
   The Bergens fired her because she stood up for Patty and "talked back" to them, telling them things they didn't want to hear.

3. What did the townspeople do to Patty?
   They called her bad names and spit at her.

4. Why did Harry need a new job?
   The townspeople would not shop at his store because he was a Nazi-lover, so he could not make a living.

5. What did Pearl expect her father to do?
   She expected him to give Harry a job.

6. Where did Patty stay after her aid to Anton was exposed?
   She stayed with her grandparents.

7. Who came to visit Patty at her grandparents' house?
   Charlene Madlee came to visit Patty.

Chapters 19-21
1. Why did Mr. Grimes stop off to get food for Patty and himself?
   The people at the school wouldn't serve Patty any food. Because he felt sorry for her, he decided to stop and get her something to eat.

2. Why couldn't Patty mention that Mr. Grimes had taken her out to eat?
    He was not supposed to stop anywhere with a prisoner. If she would mention it to anyone, he would get into trouble, and that wouldn't be a very nice payment for his kindness.

3. What was Patty's sentence?
    She was to spend 4 to 6 months at the Arkansas Reformatory for Girls.

4. What was Mr. Hollis' advice to anyone who has to go to court?
    He says to beware of at least two people--the lawyer the state hires to convict you and the lawyer you hire to defend yourself.

5. To what did Patty compare the screening on the windows?
    She compared it to the screening they use for the animals at the zoo.

6. Who is Patty's roommate?
    Her roommate is Mavis McCall.

7. What does Mavis call Patty?
    She calls her "Natz."

8. Why is Mavis in the reformatory?
    She is in for theft.

9. What set Patty apart from the rest of the girls at the reformatory?
    Patty thought her subscription to the Memphis *Commercial Appeal* set her apart.

10. Who came to visit Patty at the reformatory?
    Ruth came.

11. Who is Ruth's new boss?
    Ruth now works for the colored school teacher, Cora Mae Ford.

12. Who does Ruth say she loves the most?
    She loves Patty the most.

13. What did Ruth call Patty's parents?
    She called them "irregular seconds folks."

14. What is a "nom de plume"?
    It is a pen name.

15. What is Patty's pen name?
   Her pen name is Antonia Alexander.

16. What did Miss Laud call Patty?
   She said Patty was a greedy, spoiled girl.

17. To what did Patty compare Ruth's leaving?
   She compared Ruth's leaving to having her life raft floating out to sea.

18. What did Patty learn about herself?
   She learned that she is a person of value who could have a happy life.

MULTIPLE CHOICE STUDY GUIDE/QUIZ QUESTIONS - *Summer of My German Soldier*

Chapters 1 & 2

1. Why were the Nazis coming to Jenkinsville?
    a. They were double agents who were coming to brief the Americans on the Germans' war plans.
    b. They were prisoners of war coming to the camp located there.
    c. They were refugees seeking asylum.
    d. They all had terminal illnesses and had to be quarantined in a relatively unpopulated area.

2. True or False: Patty was disappointed upon seeing the Nazis. She thought they looked more dramatic and angry in the movies. These men just looked ordinary.
    a. True
    b. False

3. Everyone was supposed to grow food until the war was over. What name was given to this effort.
    a. It was called a Victory Garden.
    b. It was called a Patriotic Plot.
    c. It was called the Supportive Farm Effort.
    d. It was called Crops for Peace.

4. Who is Ruth?
    a. She is Patty's aunt.
    b. She is Patty's tutor.
    c. She is Patty's housekeeper.
    d. She is Patty's guardian.

5. Who is Robert?
    a. He is the chauffeur.
    b. He is the son of someone Patty knows. He was sent off to war.
    c. He is a boy in Patty's class, on whom she has a crush.
    d. He is a neighbor Patty likes to play with.

6. What is Patty's sister's name?
    a. Shelly
    b. Cherie
    c. Karen
    d. Sharon

Summer of My German Soldier Multiple Choice Study Questions Page 2

7. What was Patty's lie?
    a. Her lie was that a Nazi had tried to escape and the guard tried to stop him.
    b. Her lie was that the Germans were waving a banner of Hitler as they got off the train.
    c. Her lie was that she had spoken to the Nazis, who threatened to kill her.
    d. Her lie was that one of the Germans looked just like a boy from their town who had gone off to war the previous year and had not been heard from since.

8. What does Patty's father hate?
    a. He hates the sound of children laughing and playing.
    b. He hates to see leftover food on a plate. He expects everyone to eat everything.
    c. He hates to take a favor because he doesn't like to feel obligated.
    d. He hates to hear criticisms about his merchandise.

9. What was Mr. and Mrs. Bergen's rule about the girls taking money from their grandparents?
    a. Patty could take money because she was older and more responsible, but Sharon couldn't take any.
    b. Sharon could take money because she was little, but Patty couldn't take any.
    c. Both could accept money, but they had to turn it over to their mother.
    d. Neither was allowed to accept money.

10. How does Patty tell how grown-up Grandmas thinks she is?
    a. Grandma saves old telephone books and Sears catalogues to use as booster seats at the table. The more grown up she is, the fewer books Patty needs on top of the chair in order to be able to reach the table.
    b. Grandma only gives the children spoons and forks. It is a sign of being grown up when Patty also gets a knife as a part of the place-setting.
    c. The younger children have to wear aprons at the table. The older children don't. This time, Patty doesn't find an apron on her chair.
    d.. The more grown up she is, the more wine Grandma gives her in her glass.

11. What did Grandma say was the difference between Pearl and her brothers?
    a. Pearl was always willing to work for what she got, but the boys were not.
    b. The boys were smarter, but Pearl studied more and did better.
    c. The boys always liked what they were given, but Pearl never liked anything once it was hers.
    d. The boys were generous with their time and possessions, but Pearl was selfish.

12. True or False: When Patty leaves Memphis, she feels like she has just left home and is going to the place where she lives.
    a. True
    b. False

Summer of My German Soldier Multiple Choice Study Questions Page 3

Chapters 3 - 5

13. Why did the P.O.W.'s come to the Bergens' store?
    a. They came to get sturdy shoes.
    b. Mr. Bergen had had prison uniforms made. They were coming to try them on.
    c. It was in the Articles of War that they could buy personal supplies.
    d. They came to buy straw field hats.

14. What was different about Reiker?
    a. He was much younger than the others.
    b. He was the only one with brown eyes.
    c. He spoke English better than the others.
    d. He was belligerent, while the others seemed frightened and subdued.

15. What did Anton buy at the Bergen's store?
    a. He bought three packs of cigarettes and a lighter.
    b. He bought a pocket pencil sharpener and a gaudy pin.
    c. He bought writing paper and a fountain pen.
    d. He bought candy bars and socks.

16. What was Patty's lie to Sister Parker?
    a. She said that Anton was really a counter-spy in the service of the U.S. Government. He was posing as a prisoner to get information.
    b. She said Anton was planning a breakout.
    c. She said Anton hated Hitler more than anyone in the world and that he prayed every night that the Americans would win the war.
    d. She said that Anton had told her the prisoners were being mistreated. They had asked for her help in contacting someone who could help them file a complaint.

17. Patty sometimes went to play with Edna Louise. Who was she?
    a. She was the daughter of the richest man in town. She was always perfectly dressed and was boy crazy.
    b. She was Ruth's niece, Patty had to sneak out to play with her, because her father would not let her play with Negroes.
    c. She was an older girl whom Patty idolized. Edna felt sorry for Patty, and \ sometimes let her tag along when she went shopping or visiting other friends.
    d. She was Patty's closest friend, in whom Patty confided.

Summer of My German Soldier Multiple Choice Study Questions Page 4

18. True or False: Patty tried to punish Edna Louise by making insults about her family.
    a. True
    b. False

19. What is Patty's only ambition?
    a. She wants to get married and leave town.
    b. She wants to be beautiful and sophisticated.
    c. She wants to take dancing lessons and join a dance troupe.
    d. She wants to learn the meaning of every word in the dictionary.

20. Who does Sharon look like?
    a. She looks like her paternal grandmother.
    b. She looks like her father.
    c. She looks like her mother.
    d. She looks like a favorite aunt.

21. What did Patty and Freddy play, and what was the result of the game?
    a. They played "chase the bats." Patty ran through someone's vegetable garden and trampled the tomatoes.
    b. They played "hit the hubcap." A stone broke the window of a passing car.
    c. They played "dead." An elderly woman saw them, got frightened, and had a heart attack.
    d. They played "Nazi." The minister saw them and reprimanded them.

22. Patty describes someone's singing as not being from the throat like most people, but rather "...coming from a deeper, quieter place than that." Who is Patty describing?
    a. Ruth
    b. Sharon
    c. Her father
    d. Her grandfather

23. How did Patty's father react to her prank with Freddy?
    a. He laughed and told her to go and play some more.
    b. He grounded her for a week.
    c. He beat her.
    d. He ignored her and told her mother to handle it.

Summer of My German Soldier Multiple Choice Study Questions Page 5

Chapters 6 - 9

24. Why is Saturday Patty's favorite day of the week?
    a. She goes to see her grandmother.
    b. She has church school, and she enjoys the activities.
    c. She gets to stay in bed and read.
    d. She helps out at the store, which she enjoys.

25. True or False: Patty enjoys getting her hair done by Mrs. Reeves, the most popular hairdresser in town. She was very pleased that he mother was letting her go for a perm.
    a. True
    b. False

26. What was the reason Patty gave Mrs. Reeves for not going to Baptist training camp?
    a. There were too many mosquitoes and black moccasin snakes.
    b. She had severe allergies, and her doctor had recommended against it.
    c. She didn't like to associate with people who were not Jewish.
    d. Her parents could not afford it because the store was not doing well.

27. "Sometimes I think she's the wisest of us all. She isn't tactless...or nervous, and she doesn't get into trouble..." Who is Patty describing?
    a. Her mother
    b. Ruth
    c. Sharon
    d. Her grandmother

28. What did Patty do to the "hide out?"
    a. She painted the walls.
    b. She decorated it with pictures of movie stars.
    c. She installed a combination lock that only she could open.
    d. She cleaned it from top to bottom.

29. What did Ruth do to Patty's hair?
    a. She braided it.
    b. She cut it.
    c. She permed it.
    d. She left it alone, because she was afraid Mrs. Bergen would yell at her if she did anything to it.

Summer of My German Soldier Multiple Choice Study Questions Page 6

30. True or False: Patty saw Anton Reiker and three of the other prisoners running toward the train. The other three got on, but Anton was not able to jump quickly enough and was left behind.
    a. True
    b. False

31. True or False: Anton because angry when Patty said his name because someone might have heard her.
    a. True
    b. False

32. How did Anton escape from the POW camp?
    a. He dug a tunnel under the fence.
    b. He stole a delivery man's uniform and truck. His English was so good that no one suspected him.
    c. He bribed a guard by giving him fake diamonds to drive him out.
    d. He pretended to be sick and need medical attention. When the guard brought him into town to see the doctor, he ran away.

33. What was so ironic about Patty's helping Anton?
    a. Patty was the same age as his younger sister.
    b. His fiancée's name was also Patty.
    c. He had once helped a young refugee girl in Germany.
    d. Patty was Jewish.

34. What were the men in the town talking about?
    a. They were talking about the falling price of stocks.
    b. They were talking about the escaped prisoners.
    c. They were talking about the drought.
    d. They were talking about the President's position on the war.

35. What did Mr. Blakey think was working in the United States?
    a. He thought it was the Israeli Liberation Movement.
    b. He thought it was the Ku Klux Klan.
    c. He thought it was the Nazi underground.
    d. He thought it was the European Counterintelligence Alliance.

Summer of My German Soldier Multiple Choice Study Questions Page 7

36. Who came into the Bergen's store to investigate the disappearance of the P.O.W.?
    a. It was the Green Berets.
    b. It was the National Guard.
    c. It was the Arkansas S.W.A.T. Team.
    d. It was the F.B.I.

37. What did Patty tell the investigator was most unusual about Reiker?
    a. He was the only prisoner with dark hair.
    b. He wore a silver cross on a chain around his neck.
    c. He was very polite.
    d. He spoke English better than the others.

38. Who was Charlene Madlee?
    a. She was a newspaper reporter from the Memphis Commercial Appeal who had come to investigate the story.
    b. She was an attorney sent from the German Embassy to defend the rights of the prisoner.
    c. She was a local historian who was writing a book about the area. She thought the topic would be good to include in her book.
    d. She was an undercover Nazi agent, sent to find Anton before the Americans did.

Summer of My German Soldier Multiple Choice Study Questions Page 8

Chapters 10 - 12

39. How did Mr. Bergen and Anton react to Patty's shirt gift?
    a. They both thanked her and tried it on.
    b. Mr. Bergen said thanks and tossed it aside. Anton looked at it, felt it, and showed pleasure.
    c. Mr. Bergen yelled at her for buying from a competitor. Anton was just glad to have something to wear.
    d. Mr. Bergen ignored it. Anton liked it but was worried that Patty would get in trouble for stealing it.

40. True or False: Anton saw Mr. Bergen beating Patty for playing with Freddy. He tried to save her, but by the time he got downstairs, Mr. Bergen had already finished and had gone in the house.
    a. True
    b. False

41. Why was Mrs. Bergen angry at Ruth?
    a. She thought Ruth was stealing food from the kitchen.
    b. She thought Ruth was keeping part of the grocery money to send to her son.
    c. She thought Ruth was feeding Patty too much, and that Patty would get fat.
    a. She though Ruth was eating too much of the Bergens' food and that she should eat at home.

42. What did Patty tell her parents about the missing food?
    a. She said Sharon had given it to the neighbor's dog.
    b. She said Ruth had taken it home for her sick husband.
    c. She said she (Patty) had eaten the salami and that Sharon and Sue Ellen had eaten the chicken.
    d. She said she thought they should all become vegetarians, so she had thrown the meat out.

43. What did Ruth want Patty to tell her?
    a. Ruth wanted to know about the man in the garage.
    b. Ruth wanted to know why Patty always defied her parents.
    c. Ruth wanted to know about Mr. Bergen's childhood so she could understand why he was so mean.
    d. Ruth wanted to know if Patty really loved her parents.

Summer of My German Soldier Multiple Choice Study Questions Page 9

44. True or False: Anton told Patty that after Mr. Bergen had beaten her, he had gone to the side of the garage and cried that no one loved him.
    a. True
    b. False

45. What comparison did Anton make?
    a. He compared Patty to a suffering saint.
    b. He compared America to heaven.
    c. He compared Mr. Bergen to Hitler.
    d. He compared himself to Patrick Henry.

46. When Anton offered Ruth a chair, she acted embarrassed, just as Patty had expected her to.
    a. True
    b. False

47. What did Mr. Eugene Jackson do to Ruth's mother?
    a. He freed her from slavery.
    b. He stole the money she had put away for Ruth's education.
    c. He introduced her to her husband.
    d. He raped her, and she got pregnant with Ruth.

48. "They are both in business to give people what they think they want." Who or what is Anton comparing?
    a. He is comparing leaders and department stores.
    b. He is comparing writers and government.
    c. He is comparing churches and salesmen.
    d. He is comparing Hitler and President Roosevelt.

Summer of My German Soldier Multiple Choice Study Questions Page 10

Chapters 13 - 16

49. Why was Ruth worried?
    a. She had not heard from her son in two months.
    b. She was afraid that if she was too kind to Patty, she would get fired.
    c. She thought Anton might try to take Patty hostage in order to negotiate the release of other prisoners.
    d. She thought Patty's secret would be discovered.

50. What was Patty's plan?
    a. She would help Anton escape and then come home and act innocent.
    b. She would go with Anton.
    c. She would meet Anton in two weeks in Detroit. Then they would got to Canada.
    d. She would let him stay in the garage until the end of the war and then marry him.

51. What was Anton's last lesson for Patty?
    a. "You are a person of value and you have a friend who loved you enough to give you his most valuable possession."
    a. "Take this as a sign of my undying love. I shall return for you, no matter what it takes."
    c. "You mean more to me than life itself. You have a permanent place in my heart."
    d. "You have shown what the whole world should realize; that people of different backgrounds can indeed love and help each other."

52. What did Anton give to Patty?
    a. He gave her his family Bible, which he had hidden and carried with him.
    b. He gave her a pair of diamond earrings that had belonged to his mother.
    c. He gave her a silver money clip and one thousand dollars in American bills.
    d. He gave her a gold ring which had been in his family for generations.

53. Where did Harry think Sharon could go?
    a. He thought she could be successful in Hollywood.
    b. He though she could be a professor at a prestigious women's college.
    c. He though she could make it in the New York City fashion industry.
    d. He thought she could marry a politician and become the wife of a governor, senator, possibly even the president.

Summer of My German Soldier Multiple Choice Study Questions Page 11

54. Where did Patty tell Sister Parker she got the gift?
    a. She said she had found it in the woods near the railroad tracks.
    b. She said she had fed a tramp and that he had given her the gift out of gratitude.
    c. She said that she had been walking around the perimeter of the prison camp. One of the prisoners had thrown it over the fence and asked her to keep it.
    d. She said that she had found it in the trash dumpster in back of her father's store.

55. True or False: When Harry found out about the ring, he did not believe Patty's story. He suspected that she had let a man touch her, and got the gift as payment. Because of his belief, he beat her.
    a. True
    b. False

56. Who came to the store to talk to Patty?
    a. Rabbi Freid from Memphis came to talk to her.
    b. Mr. Kishner from the CIA came to talk to her.
    c. Sheriff Cauldwell came to talk to her.
    d. Major Jackson from the P.O.W. camp came to talk to her.

57. True or False: Patty embellished her story about the gift in order to protect herself and her family. She suddenly realized that she was being linked to Anton's disappearance.
    a. True
    b. False

58. What was Patty's one gain?
    a. She received reward money for her information.
    b. Her father respected her.
    c. She was satisfied that Anton was safe.
    d. She knew she was promoting world peace, even if only on a small scale.

59. What was Patty's loss?
    a. She had lost her innocence.
    b. She had lost the little bit of love her mother had for her.
    c. She had lost her one chance to escape from her miserable life.
    d. She had lost Anton.

Summer of My German Soldier Multiple Choice Study Questions Page 12

60. How did the FBI man link the Bergens to Anton?
- a. He had the shirt Anton had been wearing, which had Mr. Bergen's initials on it.
- a. When Anton was searched, the FBI found a letter in his pocket addressed to Patty. They read it, and were now using it as evidence.
- b. They had had secret surveillance cameras and microphones set up in and around the Bergen house. They heard Patty talking to Ruth.
- d. Anton's contact in another city, who had been arrested, knew all about Patty. He offered to tell all in return for a lighter jail sentence for himself.

61. What happened to Anton?
- a. He successfully made it out of the country.
- b. He was captured and sent back to jail.
- c. He was shot and killed while trying to escape.
- d. He asked for, and was granted, political asylum in the US.

Summer of My German Soldier Multiple Choice Study Questions Page 13

<u>Chapters 17 - 18</u>

62. What was the reason Patty gave her father for helping Anton?
    a. She wanted to prove that Jews and Germans could get along.
    b. She did it deliberately to get her parents angry.
    c. Anton had threatened to hurt the family if she didn't help him.
    d. He was kind to her, and she was being kind in return.

63. What happened to Ruth?
    a. The Bergens fired her for standing up for Patty and talking back to them.
    b. She was arrested for conspiracy, but the NAACP got her released.
    c. She moved to Detroit to live with her sister.
    d. She opened a small cafe in the Negro section of town and was very successful.

64. What did the townspeople do to Patty?
    a. They ran her out of town.
    b. They felt badly for her and tried to help her.
    c. They called her bad names and spit at her.
    d. They were angry, but they knew she was a child so they just asked her parents to keep her out of sight so she would not influence their children.

65. What happened to Harry?
    a. He had a heart attack from the stress and had to close the store.
    b. The townspeople would not shop at his store, and he could not make a living.
    c. He was so humiliated that he moved to another state and changed the family name.
    d. He sold everything he had and become an activist to help get Jews out of Germany.

66. What did Pearl expect her father to do?
    a. She expected him to let her family move in with him and his wife.
    b. She expected her father to ignore her family and was pleased when he didn't.
    c. She expected her father to give them enough money to live on for a year.
    d. She expected her father to give Harry a job.

67. Where did Patty stay after her aid to Anton was exposed?
    a. She stayed with Ruth.
    b. She stayed with her grandparents.
    c. She stayed with the Rabbi and his wife.
    d. She stayed in protective custody in the Memphis city jail.

Summer of My German Soldier Multiple Choice Study Questions Page 14

Chapters 19 - 21

68. Why did Mr. Grimes stop off to get food for Patty and himself.
    a. He felt sorry for her because he knew the people at the school would not serve her after hours.
    b. He was trying to give her a chance to escape, but she didn't realize it.
    c. He had been ordered to do so by Patty's lawyer.
    b. He had secretly arranged for a photographer to be at the restaurant. He was going to let the photographer take pictures of Patty. Then the two of them would sell the photos to a news magazine and split the profit.

69. True or False: Patty told the people at the school that Mr. Grimes had taken her out to eat.
    a. True
    b. False

70. What was Patty's sentence?
    a. She was to spend two years on probation and live with a foster family in another town.
    b. She was to spend three months doing community service at a Veteran's hospital, while undergoing weekly psychiatric treatment.
    c. She was to be sent to the P.O.W. camp until the end of the war and then would be under FBI surveillance for the rest of her life.
    d. She was to spend 4 to 6 months at the Arkansas Reformatory for Girls.

71. What was Mr. Hollis' advice to anyone to has to go to court.
    a. Always tell the truth, no matter what.
    b. Beware of two people--the lawyer the state hires to convict you and the lawyer you hire to defend yourself.
    c. Try to get a judge who is of the same religion as you are.
    d. Ask to have your case heard on a Tuesday, Wednesday, or Thursday. The judges and lawyers are tired on Mondays and are in a hurry to finish on Fridays.

72. What two things did Patty compare?
    a. She compared the attitude of the guards with that of her father.
    c. She compared what she had done to the work of the abolitionists during the Civil War.
    c. She compared the screening on the windows to the screening used for animals at the zoo.
    d. She compared military generals to inmates at an insane asylum.

Summer of My German Soldier Multiple Choice Study Questions Page 15

73. Who is Patty's roommate?
    a. Her name is Ella Hopkins.
    b. Her name is Sharon Fields.
    c. Her name is Carolyn Hammett.
    d. Her name is Mavin McCall.

74. What does her roommate call Patty?
    a. She calls her "Natz."
    b. She calls her "Patty the Unpatriotic."
    c. She calls her "Jew Killer."
    d. She calls her "Hitler's Daughter."

75. What was Patty's roommates crime?
    a. She tried to kill her parents.
    b. She was selling drugs.
    c. She committed a theft.
    d. She refused to go to school. She became so disruptive when forced to go that no one could handle her.

76. What set Patty apart from the other girls?
    a. She was the youngest.
    b. She had a subscription to the Memphis *Commercial Appeal* newspaper.
    c. She had better clothes and had food sent in from home.
    d. Her "crime" was the most famous and received much more publicity than any of the others.

77. Who came to visit Patty?
    a. Her mother came.
    b. Her grandparents came.
    c. Freddy came.
    d. Ruth came.

78. Who is Ruth's new boss?
    a. Ruth works for Patty's grandparents.
    b. Ruth works for Sister Parker.
    c. Ruth works for the colored school teacher, Cora Mae Ford.
    d. Ruth works for the NAACP.

79. True or False: Ruth says she loves her son, Robert, the most, and then Patty.
    a. True
    b. False

Summer of My German Soldier Multiple Choice Study Questions Page 16

80. What did Ruth call Patty's parents?
    a. She called them "irregular seconds folks."
    b. She called them "rich white trash."
    c. She called them "child-hating heathens."
    d. She called them "loveless vipers."

81. What is a "nom de plume?"
    a. It is the name of Patty's favorite chicken dish, which Ruth brought for her.
    b. It is a pen name, used for writing.
    c. It is the name of an angel. A boy or girl receives it when an adult wishes special blessings for them.
    d. It is a file of information that is kept on every youth under the age of eighteen who commits a crime.

82. How did Patty sign the articles she wrote?
    a. Wilhemina Bergmeister.
    b. Patricia Ginsberg.
    c. Ruth Sharon Reiker.
    d. Antonia Alexander.

83. What did Miss Laud call Patty?
    a. She called her an inspiration to the others.
    b. She called her an intellect far ahead of her years.
    c. She called her a greedy, spoiled girl.
    d. She called her a poor, misguided non-Christian.

84. To what did Patty compare Ruth's leaving?
    a. She compared it to a sunset.
    b. She compared it to having a life raft float out to sea.
    c. She compared it to a train derailing.
    d. She compared it to the birth process.

85. What did Patty learn about herself?
    a. She learned that she was a person of value who could have a happy life.
    b. She learned that she had been angry and misguided but could reform if she tried hard enough.
    c. She came to believe that there was no hope for herself.
    d. She learned that if she were mean and stubborn, she could get through any tough situation in life.

ANSWER KEY: MULTIPLE CHOICE STUDY/QUIZ QUESTIONS
Summer of My German Soldier

Chapters 1 - 2
1. B
2. A
3. A
4. C
5. B
6. D
7. A
8. C
9. B
10. D
11. C
12. A

Chapters 3 - 5
13. D
14. C
15. B
16. C
17. A
18. B
19. D
20. C
21. B
22. A
23. C

Chapters 6 - 9
24. D
25. B
26. A
27. C
28. D
29. B
30. B
31. A
32. C
33. D
34. B
35. C
36. D
37. C
38. A

Chapters 10 - 12
39. B
40. B
41. A
42. C
43. A
44. A
45. C
46. B
47. B
48. A

Chapters 13 - 16
49. D
50. B
51. A
52. D
53. A
54. B
55. A
56. C
57. B
58. B
59. D
60. A
61. C

Chapters 17 - 18
62. D
63. A
64. C
65. B
66. D
67. B

Chapters 19 - 21
68. A
69. B
70. D
71. B
72. C
73. D
74. A
75. C
76. B
77. D
78. C
79. B
80. A
81. B
82. D
83. C
84. B
85. A

PREREADING VOCABULARY WORKSHEETS

VOCABULARY - *Summer of My German Soldier*

<u>Chapters 1 - 2</u> Part I: Using Prior Knowledge and Contextual Clues

Below are the sentences in which the vocabulary words appear in the text. Read the sentence. Use any clues you can find in the sentence combined with your prior knowledge, and write what you think the underlined words mean on the lines provided.

1. As a matter of fact, if you haven't noticed, I'm really quite <u>formidable</u>.

_____

2. The nerve at his temple would <u>pulsate</u>.

_____

3. Maybe it's because he hates favors--not so much to give as to take them. "I don't like to be <u>obligated</u>," is the way he puts it.

_____

4. She looked at me <u>reproachfully</u>, like Cinderella being disturbed while waltzing with the prince.

_____

5. Now, forty years later, it has changed color and so has his expression. Then it was--<u>resolute</u>. Yes, <u>resolute</u>. And now it's just gentle.

_____

6. My father gave <u>dire</u> warnings about the Russians--how it would be better if they were fighting against us.

_____

Part II: Determining the Meaning: Match the vocabulary words to their dictionary definitions.

  ___ 1. formidable   A. indebted; owing
  ___ 2. pulsate   B. expressing blame or reprimand
  ___ 3. obligated   C. substantial
  ___ 4. reproachfully   D. expand and contract rhythmically; beat
  ___ 5. resolute   E. urgent; desperate; having terrible consequences
  ___ 6. dire   F. expressing firm determination

Vocabulary - *Summer of My German Soldier* Chapters 3 - 6

Part I: Using Prior Knowledge and Contextual Clues
   Below are the sentences in which the vocabulary words appear in the text. Read the sentence. Use any clues you can find in the sentence combined with your prior knowledge, and write what you think the underlined words mean on the lines provided.

1. My father remained impassive.

_____

2. She didn't look any way at all except in sort of neutral gear.

_____

3. She and Sue Ellen spent practically the whole day, every day, getting in and out of a water-filled galvanized tin tub. . . .

_____

4. I glanced again at the grotesque bird.

_____

5. I remembered their car. The sickly sound of it. The lackluster blackness of it.

_____

6. The pain was almost tolerable when a second blow crashed against my cheek. . . .

_____

7. But they caught all them saboteurs and that's the important thing to remember.

_____

8. Shame and anger, anger and shame mingled together, taking on something beyond the power of both.

_____

Vocabulary - *Summer of My German Soldier* Chapters 3 - 6 Continued

Part II: Determining the Meaning: Match the vocabulary words to their definitions.

___ 7. impassive   A. coated with rust-resistant zinc
___ 8. neutral   B. dull
___ 9. galvanized   C. bearable
___ 10. grotesque   D. those who take treacherous action to defeat or hinder a cause
___ 11. lackluster   E. mixed
___ 12. tolerable   F. revealing no emotion
___ 13. saboteurs   G. bizarre; distorted appearance
___ 14. mingled   H. not aligned with any side in a war, dispute or contest

Vocabulary - *Summer of My German Soldier* Chapters 7-9

Part I: Using Prior Knowledge and Contextual Clues

Below are the sentences in which the vocabulary words appear in the text. Read the sentence. Use any clues you can find in the sentence combined with your prior knowledge, and write what you think the underlined words mean on the lines provided.

1. Once I figured out that the only thing that Sharon didn't have was enough words. But I could teach her. All kinds. . . . Fat ones like *harmonic* and *palatable.*

   _____

2. The Justice Department will try the men for treason.

   _____

3. . . . these jokes, that you are making about the new regime must cease!

   _____

4. The pertinent point is that I was able to create a--a kind of climate that permitted the escape.

   _____

5. Some of our prisoners, mostly former members of the S.S., are truly fanatical men.

   _____

6. It was then that I experienced the last of my fear taking flight. Nestling down in its place came exultation.

   _____

Part II: Determining the Meaning: Match the vocabulary words to their definitions.

___ 15. palatable   A. government in power; main social structure
___ 16. treason   B. possessed with or motivated by excessive zeal
___ 17. regime   C. acceptable to the mind or senses
___ 18. pertinent   D. a feeling of triumph, happiness and joy
___ 19. fanatical   E. violations of allegiance toward one's country or cause
___ 20. exultation   F. relevant to the matter at hand

Vocabulary - *Summer of My German Soldier* Chapters 10 -12

Part I: Using Prior Knowledge and Contextual Clues
    Below are the sentences in which the vocabulary words appear in the text. Read the sentence. Use any clues you can find in the sentence combined with your prior knowledge, and write what you think the underlined words mean on the lines provided.

1. The box was cocoa-brown, and the cover came <u>embossed</u> with three golden acorns, the symbol of Oak Hall, the finest men's store in all of Memphis.

_____

2. I began to hope that his <u>exhaustion</u> would cut short the agony.

_____

3. My eyes shut in a <u>feeble</u> try at pushing away the memories.

_____

4. . . . because it seems to me that a man who is <u>incapable</u> of humor is capable of cruelty.

_____

5. Ruth's face slowly turned <u>incredulous</u>.

_____

6. "I'll pack you up some food to take with you," said Ruth with <u>unaccustomed</u> speed.

_____

Part II: Determining the Meaning: Match the vocabulary words to their definitions.

    ___ 21. embossed   A. expressive of disbelief
    ___ 22. exhaustion   B. a raised design or decoration
    ___ 23. feeble   C. not usual; something one isn't used to
    ___ 24. incapable   D. lacking the ability or power
    ___ 25. incredulous   E. fatigue
    ___ 26. unaccustomed   F. weak

Vocabulary - *Summer of My German Soldier* <u>Chapters 13 - 16</u>

Part I: Using Prior Knowledge and Contextual Clues

Below are the sentences in which the vocabulary words appear in the text. Read the sentence. Use any clues you can find in the sentence combined with your prior knowledge, and write what you think the underlined words mean on the lines provided.

1. Mr. Harry Bergen, <u>prominent</u> local merchant.

_____

2. "Did he say what you're 'pose to do with your burdens? They got pills in Boston for that?" When she gets <u>sarcastic</u> there's not much I can think to say to her.

_____

3. I needed to say his name aloud again as though it were a magical <u>incantation</u>.

_____

4. "Oh, yes, ma'am," I said, trying to put real <u>conviction</u> in my voice.

_____

5. ". . . After all, work should have <u>relevance</u>," I said borrowing one of Anton's words.

_____

6. . . . whatever he may say or do, I'm going to survive pretty much <u>intact</u>.

_____

7. Then it hit me that what I had asked for might come under the heading of <u>blasphemy</u> . . . .

_____

Part II: Determining the Meaning: Match the vocabulary words to their definitions.

___ 27. prominent   A. chant or charm
___ 28. sarcastic   B. applicability to social issues
___ 29. incantation   C. widely known
___ 30. conviction   D. remaining whole or uninjured
___ 31. relevance   E. expressing cutting or ironic remarks
___ 32. intact   F. speaking of or to God in an irreverent way
___ 33. blasphemy   G. characteristic of being convincing or believable

Vocabulary - *Summer of My German Soldier* Chapters 17 - 18

Part I: Using Prior Knowledge and Contextual Clues

Below are the sentences in which the vocabulary words appear in the text. Read the sentence. Use any clues you can find in the sentence combined with your prior knowledge, and write what you think the underlined words mean on the lines provided.

1. But I can see him still, his face contorted.

_____

2. My father looked as though I had just finished telling him the world's most incredible lie.

_____

3. As we came to my father's store, I saw people milling in front.

_____

4. "You people are obstructing justice," said Pierce.

_____

5. Well, Mr. Hammett had lunch with a high official from the Justice Department, which would be the agency responsible for initiating legal actions in such cases as Patty's.

_____

6. "It's only the slightest of possibilities," said Charlene slowly, as though she were choosing her words with inordinate care.

_____

Part II: Determining the Meaning: Match the vocabulary words to their definitions.

___ 34. contorted   A. beginning
___ 35. incredible   B. hindering; blocking
___ 36. milling   C. more than is usual; extraordinary
___ 37. obstructing   D. unbelievable
___ 38. initiating   E. twisted out of shape
___ 39. inordinate   F. moving around without any particular direction

Vocabulary - *Summer of My German Soldier* Chapters 19 - 21

Part I: Using Prior Knowledge and Contextual Clues
    Below are the sentences in which the vocabulary words appear in the text. Read the sentence. Use any clues you can find in the sentence combined with your prior knowledge, and write what you think the underlined words mean on the lines provided.

1. As the road turned off to the left, there was a definite rise from the flatness of the delta lands. Beginning in me was a matching feeling of <u>ascent</u>.

   _____

2. Mr. Grimes' dry voice popped my bubble of <u>reverie</u>.

   _____

3. Ashes and cigarette butts filled the glass ash tray to <u>capacity</u>.

   _____

4. I measured the <u>bleakness</u> of the morning against the painted grayness of the walls and estimated the time to be six thirty.

   _____

5. The girls had all gone over to the <u>nondenominational</u> services in the chapel.

   _____

6. It was what I said next that made me hesitate because it sounded <u>presumptuous</u>.

   _____

7. I got the Antonia from Anton, and I picked Alexander because of the <u>alliteration</u>, both names starting with the same letter.

   _____

8. She clicked open her <u>simulated</u> alligator pocketbook, giving me a view of the inside.

   _____

Vocabulary - *Summer of My German Soldier* Chapters 19-21 Continued

Part II: Determining the Meaning: Match the vocabulary words to their definitions.

___ 40. ascent
___ 41. reverie
___ 42. capacity
___ 43. bleakness
___ 44. nondenominational
___ 45. presumptuous
___ 46. alliteration
___ 47. simulated

A. excessively forward
B. general; having no ties to a specific religion
C. gloominess; dreariness
D. daydream
E. the limit of ability to hold something
F. upward movement; rising spirits
G. imitation
H. the repetition of the same sounds at the beginning of words

ANSWER KEY - VOCABULARY
Summer of My German Soldier

Chapters 1 - 2
1. C
2. D
3. A
4. B
5. F
6. E

Chapters 3 - 6
7. F
8. H
9. A
10. G
11. B
12. C
13. D
14. E

Chapters 7 - 9
15. C
16. E
17. A
18. F
19. B
20. D

Chapters 10 - 12
21. B
22. E
23. F
24. D
25. A
26. C

Chapters 13 - 16
27. C
28. E
29. A
30. G
31. B
32. D
33. F

Chapters 17 - 18
34. E
35. D
36. F
37. B
38. A
39. C

Chapters 19 - 21
40. F
41. D
42. E
43. C
44. B
45. A
46. H
47. G

DAILY LESSONS

LESSON ONE

Objectives
1. To introduce the *Summer of My German Soldier* unit
2. To distribute books and other related materials
3. To preview the study questions for chapters 1-2
4. To familiarize students with the vocabulary for chapters 1-2

NOTE: Prior to this lesson you need to have prepared a bulletin board with background paper and a title: Summer of My German Soldier : A PERSONAL VIEW OF WORLD WAR II. (If you do not have a bulletin board, use a big sheet of paper put over the chalk board or a flip-chart style paper on an easel.) Find and cut out or trace with your opaque projector pictures from World War II to add interest to the board.

Activity #1
Have each student in the class write one fact about World War II on the bulletin board using different colored markers. If you have a small class and/or students know a lot about WWII, go around the room twice to give each student two opportunities to write facts.

TRANSITION: Some students have probably written something about Nazis or concentration camps. Using their comments, go on to say something like, "Judging from your comments, you know that the Nazis were very much against the Jews and did everything they could to wipe out the Jewish race. It would seem very unlikely, then, that any Jewish person in the world would do anything to help any German, especially a Nazi, during the war. But, in fact, that is just what happens in the story we are going to read."

Activity #2
Distribute the materials students will use in this unit. Explain in detail how students are to use these materials.

Study Guides   Students should read the study guide questions for each reading assignment prior to beginning the reading assignment to get a feeling for what events and ideas are important in the section they are about to read. After reading the section, students will (as a class or individually) answer the questions to review the important events and ideas from that section of the book. Students should keep the study guides as study materials for the unit test.

Vocabulary   Prior to reading a reading assignment, students will do vocabulary work related to the section of the book they are about to read. Following the completion of the reading of the book, there will be a vocabulary review of all the words used in the vocabulary assignments. Students should keep their vocabulary work as study materials for the unit test.

Reading Assignment Sheet   You need to fill in the reading assignment sheet to let students know by when their reading has to be completed. You can either write the assignment sheet up on a side blackboard or bulletin board and leave it there for students to see each day, or you can "ditto" copies for each student to have. In either case, you should advise students to become very familiar with the reading assignments so they know what is expected of them.

Extra Activities Center   The Extra Activities page of this unit contains suggestions for an extra library of related books and articles in your classroom as well as crossword and word search puzzles. Make an extra activities center in your room where you will keep these materials for students to use. (Bring the books and articles in from the library and keep several copies of the puzzles on hand.) Explain to students that these materials are available for students to use when they finish reading assignments or other class work early.

Nonfiction Assignment Sheet   Explain to students that they each are to read at least one non-fiction piece from the in-class library at some time during the unit. Students will fill out a nonfiction assignment sheet after completing the reading to help you evaluate their reading experiences and to help the students think about and evaluate their own reading experiences.

Books   Each school has its own rules and regulations regarding student use of school books. Advise students of the procedures that are normal for your school.

Activity #3
Preview the study questions and have students do the vocabulary work for Chapters 1-2 of *Summer of My German Soldier*. If students do not finish this assignment during this class period, they should complete it prior to the next class meeting.

NONFICTION ASSIGNMENT SHEET
(To be completed after reading the required nonfiction article)

Name _____ Date _____

Title of Nonfiction Read _____

Written By _____ Publication Date _____

I. Factual Summary: Write a short summary of the piece you read.

II. Vocabulary
1. With which vocabulary words in the piece did you encounter some degree of difficulty?

2. How did you resolve your lack of understanding with these words?

III. Interpretation: What was the main point the author wanted you to get from reading his work?

IV. Criticism
1. With which points of the piece did you agree or find easy to accept? Why?

2. With which points of the piece did you disagree or find difficult to believe? Why?

V. Personal Response: What do you think about this piece? OR How does this piece influence your ideas?

LESSON TWO

Objectives
1. To read chapters 1-2
2. To give students practice reading orally
3. To evaluate students' oral reading
4. To preview and read chapters 3-5

Activity #1

Have students read chapters 1-2 of *Summer of My German Soldier* out loud in class. You probably know the best way to get readers with your class; pick students at random, ask for volunteers, or use whatever method works best for your group. If you have not yet completed an oral reading evaluation for your students this marking period, this would be a good opportunity to do so. A form is included with this unit for your convenience.

Activity #2

Tell students that prior to your next class meeting they should have completed previewing the study questions, doing the prereading vocabulary worksheet, and reading for chapters 3-5.

LESSON THREE

Objectives
1. To review the main events and ideas from chapters 1-5
2. To preview the study questions for chapter 6
3. To familiarize students with the vocabulary in chapter 6
4. To read chapter 6
5. To preview the study questions and vocabulary for chapters 7-9

Activity #1

Give students a few minutes to formulate answers for the study guide questions for chapters 1-5 and then discuss the answers to the questions in detail. Write the answers on the board or overhead transparency so students can have the correct answers for study purposes. NOTE: It is a good practice in public speaking and leadership skills for individual students to take charge of leading the discussions of the study questions. Perhaps a different student could go to the front of the class and lead the discussion each day that the study questions are discussed during this unit. Of course, the teacher should guide the discussion when appropriate and be sure to fill in any gaps the students leave.

Activity #2

Give students about fifteen minutes to preview the study questions for chapter 6 of *Summer of My German Soldier* and to do the related vocabulary work. Tell students to read chapter 6 and to do the prereading work for chapters 7-9 of *Summer of My German Soldier* prior to your next class period. If there is time remaining in this period, students may begin reading silently.

ORAL READING EVALUATION - *Summer of My German Soldier*

Name _____ Class____ Date _____

SKILL	EXCELLENT	GOOD	AVERAGE	FAIR	POOR
Fluency	5	4	3	2	1
Clarity	5	4	3	2	1
Audibility	5	4	3	2	1
Pronunciation	5	4	3	2	1
_____	5	4	3	2	1
_____	5	4	3	2	1

Total _____   Grade _____

Comments:

LESSON FOUR

Objectives
    1. To read chapters 7-9
    2. To complete the oral reading evaluations

Activity

    Have students read chapters 7-9 during this class period. If you have not yet completed the oral reading evaluations, this would be a good time to do so. If you have completed them, students may either read orally or silently (teacher's choice).

LESSON FIVE

Objectives
    1. To review the main ideas and events from chapters 6-9
    2. To give students the opportunity to practice writing to express personal opinions
    3. To give the teacher the opportunity to evaluate students' writing skills

Activity #1

    Give students a few minutes to formulate answers to the study guide questions for chapters 6-9. Discuss the answers to the questions in detail.

Activity #2

    Distribute Writing Assignment #1 and discuss the directions in detail. Allow the remaining class time for students to complete the assignment. Collect the papers at the end of the class period.

    Follow-up: After you have graded the assignments, have a writing conference with the students. After the writing conference, allow students to revise their papers using your suggestions and corrections. Give them about three days from the date they receive their papers to complete the revision. I suggest grading the revisions on an A-C-E scale (all revisions well-done, some revisions made, few or no revisions made). This will speed your grading time and still give some credit for the students' efforts.

WRITING ASSIGNMENT #1 - *Summer of My German Soldier*

PROMPT

In one sense, *Summer of My German Soldier* is mostly the story of one girl's summer vacation. That topic is probably one of the oldest writing assignments in the history of American education, but it is a good one. Your assignment is to tell about your most interesting summer vacation--or any time that something interesting happened to you or your family. Your assignment could be a regular essay-type composition, or you may choose to write in a short story format. (You won't have time to write a novel, but if you do a good job on your short story, maybe one day you would expand it to a novel!) The way in which you write your story is as important (or perhaps is more important) than the actual content of the story. It could be the usual, boring, "we did this and then we did that" kind of a composition, or it could be as interestingly written as *Summer of My German Soldier*.

PREWRITING

You probably already have an idea or two for a topic, but if you don't, think back and recall some of the most unusual things that have happened to you and/or your family. Choose a story you enjoy telling. That will make writing it easier. Jot down a few notes or a little outline of what you need to include in your story.

DRAFTING

Giving specific directions for drafting your composition is impossible since you may choose one of two formats. However, whichever format you choose, you should make sure the events and points you make are easy to follow and flow logically from one point to another. Make sure the reader has all the information he/she needs in order to understand and appreciate your story.

PROMPT

When you finish the rough draft of your paper, ask a student who sits near you to read it. After reading your rough draft, he/she should tell you what he/she liked best about your work, which parts were difficult to understand, and ways in which your work could be improved. Reread your paper considering your critic's comments and make the corrections you think are necessary.

PROOFREADING

Do a final proofreading of your paper double-checking your grammar, spelling, organization, and the clarity of your ideas.

LESSON SIX

Objectives
1. To preview the study questions and vocabulary for chapters 10-12
2. To read chapters 10-12

Activity #1
Give students about ten minutes to complete the prereading work for chapters 10-12.

Activity #2
Have students read chapters 10-12 in class. If you have not yet completed the oral reading evaluations, this would be a good time to do so. If students do not complete reading chapters 10-12 in class, they should read them independently prior to the next class period.

LESSON SEVEN

Objectives
1. To review the main events of chapters 10-12
2. To assign the prereading, vocabulary and reading work for chapters 13-16
3. To read chapters 13-16

Activity #1
Give students a few minutes to formulate answers to the study guide questions for chapters 10-12. Discuss the answers to the questions in detail.

Activity #2
Tell students that prior to their next class meeting, they should have completed the prereading and reading work for chapters 13-16. Give students this class period to work on this assignment.

LESSON EIGHT

Objectives
1. To review the main ideas of chapters 13-16
2. To preview and read chapters 17-18
3. To give students the opportunity to practice writing to inform
4. To give the teacher the opportunity to evaluate students' writing
5. To review some events and ideas from the story

Activity #1
Give students a few minutes to formulate answers to the study questions for chapters 13-16. Discuss the answers to the questions in detail.

Activity #2
Tell students that prior to your next class meeting they should have completed the prereading and reading work for chapters 17-18. Students may begin this assignment if they finish Activity #3, the writing assignment, before the end of this class period.

Activity #3
Distribute Writing Assignment #2. Discuss the directions in detail and give students ample time to complete the assignment.

LESSON NINE

Objectives
1. To review the main ideas and events from chapters 17-18
2. To preview and read chapters 19-21

Activity #1
Give students a few minutes to formulate answers to the study questions for chapters 17-18. Discuss the answers to the questions in detail.

Activity #2
Tell students that prior to your next class meeting they should have completed the prereading and reading work for chapters 19-21.

WRITING ASSIGNMENT #2 - *Summer of My German Soldier*

PROMPT
A few paragraphs from the end of chapter 7, Patty says, "Once I figured out that the only thing that Sharon didn't have was enough words. But I could teach her. . . . And when Sharon knew enough words she could teach me all those things she was born knowing."

The words chosen as examples in that paragraph can all be related to the story. Your assignment is to explain how each of those words can relate to the story *Summer of My German Soldier*.

PREWRITING
Make a list of the words on a scratch sheet of paper. Next to each word, jot down a few notes about ways in which that word could relate to the story.

DRAFTING
Write one good paragraph (at least) about each of the words, explaining how each relates to the story. Use examples and events from the text to support your ideas.

PROMPT
When you finish the rough draft of your paper, ask a student who sits near you to read it. After reading your rough draft, he/she should tell you what he/she liked best about your work, which parts were difficult to understand, and ways in which your work could be improved. Reread your paper considering your critic's comments and make the corrections you think are necessary.

PROOFREADING
Do a final proofreading of your paper double-checking your grammar, spelling, organization, and the clarity of your ideas.

LESSONS TEN AND ELEVEN

Objectives
    1. To review the main ideas and events from chapters 19-21
    2. To discuss the story on interpretive and critical levels
    3. To discuss the significance of several quotations from the story

Activity #1

    Give students a few minutes to formulate answers to the study questions for chapters 19-21. Discuss the answers to those questions in detail.

Activity #2

    Choose the questions from the Extra Discussion Questions/Writing Assignments which seem most appropriate for your students. A class discussion of these questions is most effective if students have been given the opportunity to formulate answers to the questions prior to the discussion. To this end, you may either have all the students formulate answers to all the questions, divide your class into groups and assign one or more questions to each group, or assign one question to each student in your class. The option you choose will make a difference in the amount of class time needed for this activity.

    After students have had ample time to formulate answers to the questions, begin your class discussion of the questions and the ideas presented by the questions. Be sure students take notes during the discussion so they have information to study for the unit test.

EXTRA WRITING ASSIGNMENTS/DISCUSSION QUESTIONS
Summer of My German Soldier

Interpretation

1. From what point of view is *Summer of My German Soldier* written, and what effect does that have on the story?

2. Is the *Summer of My German Soldier* believable? Explain why or why not.

3. Where is the climax of the story? Explain your choice.

4. Are the characters in *Summer of My German Soldier* stereotypes? If so, explain the usefulness of employing stereotypes in the novel. If they are not, explain how they merit individuality.

5. What is the setting of the story? Could this story have been set in a different time and place and still have the same effect?

6. What are the main conflicts in the story and how are they resolved?

Critical

6. Describe the relationships between the following people:

Patty and her father	Patty and her mother
Patty and Anton	Patty and her grandmother
Patty and Ruth	Patty and Edna Louise
Patty and Sharon	Patty and Freddy
Mr. and Mrs. Bergen	Mrs. Bergen and her mother
Mr. and Mrs. Bergen & Sharon	

7. Are Patty's actions believably motivated? Explain why or why not.

8. Characterize Bette Greene's style of writing. How does it contribute to the value of the novel?

9. Why is Patty insulted by the comparison Edna Louise makes when she says that going out with Robert is "like going out with a nigger"?

10. Why did Mr. Bergen call the sheriff to talk to Patty after he discovered the ring?

11. Are the characters in the story stereotypes? If so, explain the usefulness of employing stereotypes in the novel. If not, explain how they merit individuality.

Summer of My German Soldier Extra Discussion Questions page 2

12. "Now you listen here, Mr. FBI . . . That's no little kid, never has been, 'cause when she was born her brain was bigger than yours is now." Was it possible that Mr. Bergen was paying Patty a compliment?

13. When and why does Patty lie? Give specific examples.

17. What does Patty learn during the course of the summer (by the end of the story)?

18. What can we learn from observing Patty, her family, and the townspeople?

19. How did the townspeople react to Patty and her family after Patty's "crime" was made public? Why?

20. Patty's grandmother excused Patty's helping the man, saying Patty didn't know he was an escaped POW. Should it have made any difference whether or not Patty knew he was an escaped POW? Why or why not?

21. What does the character of Ruth add to the story?

22. Ruth said, "Mostly things don't get no better for old colored ladies." What did she mean?

23. Why did Bette Greene "kill off" Anton?

24. What "careless" things did Patty do which eventually caused her to be caught?

25. Explain the role of religion in the story.

26. Compare and contrast Anton's mother with Patty's.

Personal Response

27. Did you enjoy reading *Summer of My German Soldier*? Why or why not?

28. Was Patty's punishment appropriate? Why or why not?

29. Were Patty's parents "good" parents? What are the characteristics of "good" parents?

30. Define "prejudice" and give several examples of it from the story.

31. Have you read other stories about World War II? What were they? How were they like or different from *Summer of My German Soldier*?

Summer of My German Soldier Extra Discussion Questions page 3

Quotations

1. "Christian prayers in my house!" The nerve at his temple would pulsate. Shouts of "God damn you," directed at me and maybe at Ruth. (1)

2. "Could you tell this old lady why you is always talking about your father when all the other young girls be talking about their daddies?" (1)

3. "Ruth did not tell me to wear this dress," I said, hating the idea of being anybody's robot. Even Ruth's. (1)

4. The secret is in absolutely refusing to let the river beat you down. If I had to, I'd measure my progress in inches. One more inch I've swum--one less inch to swim. Once you know the secret, then nobody's river can bring you down." (2)

5. For a moment I thought I might come right out and ask her if she had liked my letter too, but I didn't. I didn't want to give her the impression that her opinion was all that important to me. (2)

6. "It is too. God is on America's side and anybody who's against us is on the devil's side, and that's the truth." (4)

7. I thought about all the trouble I could get into over Anton. My father would beat me, and if other people found out they'd never speak to me again unless it was to call me bad names. (7)

8. "I don't feel guilty." His hand rubbed across the slight indentation in his chin. "His concern was for reward; mine was for survival." (8)

Summer of My German Soldier Extra Discussion Questions page 4

9. "It's truly extraordinary," he said. "Who would believe it? 'Jewish girl risks all for German soldier.' Tell me, Patty Bergen--" his voice became soft, but with a trace of hoarseness--"why are you doing this for me?"
    It wasn't complicated. Why didn't he know? There was really only one word for it. A simple little word that in itself is reason enough. (8)

10. "Well, it's all mixed up with curiosity. When I read a book, I want to understand precisely what it is the writer is saying, not just almost but precisely. And it's the same when people are talking to you. . . ." (9)

11. And now that I had of my own free will broken faith with my father and my country, I felt like a good and worthy person. (10)

12. "You only get what you pay for." (10)

13. "I don't understand. Why? How could he be so mean and then worry that he isn't loved? It doesn't make sense." (11)

14. Anton looked thoughtful. "Cruelty is after all cruelty, and the difference between the two men may have more to do with their degrees of power than their degrees of cruelty." (11)

15. "There are those who would agree with you. But leaders don't usually spring forth to impose their will upon a helpless people. They, like department stores, are in business to give people what they think they want. So basically you always come back to people. How do you make better people?" (12)

Summer of My German Soldier Extra Discussion Questions page 5

16. "You don't believe in religion or education or psychiatry," I said, holding up three fingers. "Is there anything at all you do believe in?"
    ". . . I believe that love is better than hate. And that there is more nobility in building a chicken coop than in destroying a cathedral." (12)

17. I saw Sharon's Baby Jane doll lying face down beneath the rainspout. "And I love you, love you, love you, little baby." (13)

18. "Oh, you're weak, Edna Louise," I whispered to the ring. "And you're no person of value either." (14)

19. He knows that I'm an Esmeralda too for, whatever he may say or do, I'm going to survive pretty much intact." (16)

20. "Just being in the same room with you, Mother, is like being feast for a thousand starving insects." (16)

21. "He was good to me." (17)

22. "Does a person have to ask for credentials before they can give food to a hungry man? Are you responsible because you gave nourishment to a bad man? (18)

23. "When people's emotions are involved they don't want to listen." (18)

24. ". . . She's only twelve, so she didn't act wisely, O.K. But she meant good, you have to admit that." (18)

Summer of My German Soldier Extra Discussion Questions page 6

25. ". . . but do you think that if we were Protestants there would be all this hullabaloo?" (18)

26. . . . and I wondered if a blessing is still a blessing if it lasts for only a little while? (19)

27. But if Mr. Grimes calls me a prisoner, I guess he ought to know. Funny, the word has no sting. But then nothing has much sting anymore. (19)

28. "That's all they ever think about--handling me, controlling me! Why can't they just let me be?" (20)

29. "But you've got yourself some irregular seconds folks, and you've been paying more'n top dollar for them. So jest don't go a-wishing for what ain't nevah gonna be." (20)

30. It was like watching my very own life raft floating away towards the open sea. And yet somewhere in my mind's eye I thought I could see the faintest outline of land. Then it came to me that maybe that's the only thing life rafts are supposed to do. Taking the shipwrecked, not exactly to the land, but only in view of land. The final mile being theirs alone to swim." (21)

LESSON TWELVE

Objective
To review all of the vocabulary work done in this unit

Activity
Choose one (or more) of the vocabulary review activities listed below and spend your class period as directed in the activity. Some of the materials for these review activities are located in the Vocabulary Resources section in this unit.

VOCABULARY REVIEW ACTIVITIES

1. Divide your class into two teams and have an old-fashioned spelling or definition bee.

2. Give each of your students (or students in groups of two, three or four) a *Summer of My German Soldier* Vocabulary Word Search Puzzle. The person (group) to find all of the vocabulary words in the puzzle first wins.

3. Give students a *Summer of My German Soldier* Vocabulary Word Search Puzzle without the word list. The person or group to find the most vocabulary words in the puzzle wins.

4. Use a *Summer of My German Soldier* Vocabulary Crossword Puzzle. Put the puzzle onto a transparency on the overhead projector (so everyone can see it), and do the puzzle together as a class.

5. Give students a *Summer of My German Soldier* Vocabulary Matching Worksheet to do.

6. Divide your class into two teams. Use the *Summer of My German Soldier* vocabulary words with their letters jumbled as a word list. Student 1 from Team A faces off against Student 1 from Team B. You write the first jumbled word on the board. The first student (1A or 1B) to unscramble the word wins the chance for his/her team to score points. If 1A wins the jumble, go to student 2A and give him/her a definition. He/she must give you the correct spelling of the vocabulary word which fits that definition. If he/she does, Team A scores a point, and you give student 3A a definition for which you expect a correctly spelled matching vocabulary word. Continue giving Team A definitions until some team member makes an incorrect response. An incorrect response sends the game back to the jumbled-word face off, this time with students 2A and 2B. Instead of repeating giving definitions to the first few students of each team, continue with the student after the one who gave the last incorrect response on the team. For example, if Team B wins the jumbled-word face-off, and student 5B gave the last incorrect answer for Team B, you would start this round of definition questions with student 6B, and so on. The team with the most points wins!

7. Have students write a story in which they correctly use as many vocabulary words as possible. Have students read their compositions orally. Post the most original compositions on your bulletin board.

LESSONS THIRTEEN AND FOURTEEN

Objectives
1. To have students consider some career possibilities
2. To have students practice their researching skills
3. To give students the opportunity to work together in a small group

NOTE: Unlike Patty, students often will have no idea about what they want to do with their lives after they graduate from school. This assignment is designed to help students discover what career possibilities exist. All the careers listed relate to *Summer of My German Soldier*. You may add others if you wish or keep doing this assignment over and over again with different occupations related to different works of literature you read throughout the year.

Activity #1
Divide your class into six groups. Assign each group one large area of careers to research:
1. Journalism - tv news anchor, newspaper reporter, printer, etc.
2. Retail business opportunities - store owner, salesman, etc.
3. Military - air force, army, coast guard, etc.
4. Law enforcement - police, detective, guard, etc.
5. Law - attorney, judge, bailiff, court reporter, etc.
6. Education - classroom teacher, tutor, materials writer, school nurse, etc.

Give the group 10 minutes to think of specific careers within the larger category. Each group should brainstorm enough careers so that each member of the group has one specific career to research. Some examples follow the group topics above.

Activity #2
Take the students to the library or to the guidance center to get information about each specific career. Each student should find the same basic information: career title, expected and possible income, chance for advancement, job description, working hours, working conditions, education needed, skills needed, and pluses and minuses to the occupation.
A form for students to fill out is enclosed for your convenience.

Activity #3
Call on each student (by group) to orally give the information he/she collected.

Activity #4
Collect students' career information for grading. Ask your guidance personnel if they would like to have copies of the information collected to keep on file for other students in the school to use. If your classes do this assignment for each work of literature you do, they will get many ideas as to what careers are available and your guidance office will have a great file of compiled information (particularly if you use the form enclosed so everyone writes their information in the same format).

CAREER WORKSHEET

Group # _____ General Topic _____ Specific Career _____

Job Description _____
_____
_____
_____

Education Needed _____

Skills Needed _____
_____

Working Place & Working Conditions _____
_____
_____

Expected Income _____ Possible Income _____

Chances For Advancement _____
_____

Usual Working Hours _____
_____

Pluses About The Occupation _____
_____
_____

Minuses About The Occupation _____
_____
_____

Misc. Information Found _____
_____
_____
_____

LESSON FIFTEEN

Objectives
    1. To give students the opportunity to practice writing to persuade
    2. To give the teacher the opportunity to evaluate students' writing skills

Activity

    Distribute Writing Assignment #3. Discuss the directions in detail and give students ample time to complete the assignment.

While students are working on this assignment, call individual students to your desk or some other private area for individual writing conferences based on writing assignments one and two. An evaluation form is included with this unit to help you structure your conferences.

LESSON SIXTEEN

Objectives
    1. To widen the breadth of students' knowledge about the topics discussed or touched upon in *Summer of My German Soldier*
    2. To check students' nonfiction reading assignments

Activity

    Ask each student to give a brief oral report about the nonfiction work he/she read for the nonfiction reading assignment. Your criteria for evaluating this report will vary depending on the level of your students. You may wish for students to give a complete report without using notes of any kind, or you may want students to read directly from a written report, or you may want to do something in between these two extremes. Just make students aware of your criteria in ample time for them to prepare their reports.

    Start with one student's report. After that, ask if anyone else in the class has read on a topic related to the first student's report. If no one has, choose another student at random. After each report, be sure to ask if anyone has a report related to the one just completed. That will help keep a continuity during the discussion of the reports.

LESSON SEVENTEEN

Objective
   To review the main ideas presented in *Summer of My German Soldier*

Activity #1
   Choose one of the review games/activities included in the section and spend your class period as outlined there. Some materials for these activities are located in the Unit Resource section of this unit.

Activity #2
   Remind students that the Unit Test will be in the next class meeting. Stress the review of the Study Guides and their class notes as a last-minute, brush-up review for homework.

WRITING ASSIGNMENT #3 - *Summer of My German Soldier*

PROMPT

On one hand, Patty helped a POW try to escape. On the other hand, she simply gave food and shelter to another human being who was stuck in a bad situation. Was what Patty did right or wrong? Prepare a case for either her prosecution or defense at the trial.

PREWRITING

The first thing you have to do is make up your own mind whether you think what she did was right or wrong. Choose whether you want to prosecute her or defend her.

Make a list of all the reasons why she should be punished (if you are prosecuting) or let go (if you are defending). Next to each reason, make notes about what evidence from the book as well as laws and generally accepted rules in our society you will use to support your statements.

DRAFTING

Write as if you are giving your opening or closing statement to the jury at the trial.

Begin with an introductory paragraph. In the body of your composition write one paragraph for each of your reasons, filling out each paragraph with examples, evidence, and other supporting data or ideas. End with a concluding paragraph in which you sum up your arguments.

PROMPT

When you finish the rough draft of your paper, ask a student who sits near you to read it. After reading your rough draft, he/she should tell you what he/she liked best about your work, which parts were difficult to understand, and ways in which your work could be improved. Reread your paper considering your critic's comments and make the corrections you think are necessary.

PROOFREADING

Do a final proofreading of your paper double-checking your grammar, spelling, organization, and the clarity of your ideas.

WRITING EVALUATION FORM - *Summer of My German Soldier*

Name _____ Date _____

Grade _____

Circle One For Each Item:

Grammar: corrections noted on paper

Spelling: corrections noted on paper

Punctuation: corrections noted on paper

Legibility: excellent good fair poor

Strengths:

Weaknesses:

Comments/Suggestions:

REVIEW GAMES/ACTIVITIES - *Summer of My German Soldier*

1. Ask the class to make up a unit test for *Summer of My German Soldier*. The test should have 4 sections: matching, true/false, short answer, and essay. Students may use 1/2 period to make the test and then swap papers and use the other 1/2 class period to take a test a classmate has devised (open book). You may want to use the unit test included in this section or take questions from the students' unit tests to formulate your own test.

2. Take 1/2 period for students to make up true and false questions (including the answers). Collect the papers and divide the class into two teams. Draw a big tic-tac-toe board on the chalk board. Make one team X and one team O. Ask questions to each side, giving each student one turn. If the question is answered correctly, that students' team's letter (X or O) is placed in the box. If the answer is incorrect, no mark is placed in the box. The object is to get three marks in a row like tic-tac-toe. You may want to keep track of the number of games won for each team.

3. Take 1/2 period for students to make up questions (true/false and short answer). Collect the questions. Divide the class into two teams. You'll alternate asking questions to individual members of teams A & B (like in a spelling bee). The question keeps going from A to B until it is correctly answered, then a new question is asked. A correct answer does not allow the team to get another question. Correct answers are +2 points; incorrect answers are -1 point.

4. Have students pair up and quiz each other from their study guides and class notes.

5. Give students a *Summer of My German Soldier* crossword puzzle to complete.

6. Divide your class into two teams. Use the *Summer of My German Soldier* crossword words with their letters jumbled as a word list. Student 1 from Team A faces off against Student 1 from Team B. You write the first jumbled word on the board. The first student (1A or 1B) to unscramble the word wins the chance for his/her team to score points. If 1A wins the jumble, go to student 2A and give him/her a clue. He/she must give you the correct word which matches that clue. If he/she does, Team A scores a point, and you give student 3A a clue for which you expect another correct response. Continue giving Team A clues until some team member makes an incorrect response. An incorrect response sends the game back to the jumbled-word face off, this time with students 2A and 2B. Instead of repeating giving clues to the first few students of each team, continue with the student after the one who gave the last incorrect response on the team. For example, if Team B wins the jumbled-word face-off, and student 5B gave the last incorrect answer for Team B, you would start this round of clue questions with student 6B, and so on. The team with the most points wins!

UNIT TESTS

SHORT ANSWER UNIT TEST 1 - *Summer of My German Soldier*

I. Matching/Identify

___ 1. Anton   A. Patty's father

___ 2. Sharon   B. Ruth's son

___ 3. Edna Louise   C. Helped Reiker

___ 4. Ruth   D. Hairdresser

___ 5. Harry   E. Said, "God is on America's side . . ."

___ 6. Robert   F. Sheriff

___ 7. Patty   G. German soldier

___ 8. Madlee   H. Reporter

___ 9. Freddy   I. Bergen's nanny/maid

___ 10. Reeves   J. Patty's roommate

___ 11. Cauldwell   K. Patty's little sister

___ 12. Mavis   L. Boy Patty is forbidden to play with

___ 13. Antonia   M. Patty's pen name

Summer of My German Soldier Short Answer Unit Test 1 Page 2

II. Short Answer

1. Why were the Nazis coming to Jenkinsville?

2. What did Grandma say was the difference between Pearl and her brothers?

3. Why did the P.O.W.s come to the Bergens' store?

4. What was Patty's lie to Sister Parker?

5. What is Patty's only admitted ambition?

6. What is Patty's opinion of Sharon?

7. What was Mr. Bergen's reaction to Patty's shirt gift? Anton's reaction to the same gift?

8. To whom did Anton compare Mr. Bergen?

9. What did Anton give to Patty?

10. Why did Harry beat Patty at the store?

Summer of My German Soldier Short Answer Unit Test 1 Page 3

11. Why did Patty embellish her story about the tramp by telling the sheriff that the tramp had said "I could go through this world proud and happy if only God had seen it fit to give me a daughter exactly like you"?

12. What evidence did the F.B.I. man produce to link the Bergens to Anton?

13. What happened to Anton?

14. What was Patty's sentence?

15. Who came to visit Patty at the reformatory?

16. To what did Patty compare Ruth's leaving?

17. What did Patty learn about herself?

Summer of My German Soldier Short Answer Unit Test 1 Page 4

III. Composition

    What is the point of *Summer of My German Soldier*? When we read books, we usually come away from our reading experience a little richer, having given more thought to a particular aspect of life. What do you think Bette Greene intended us to gain from reading her novel?

Summer of My German Soldier Short Answer Unit Test 1 Page 5

IV. Vocabulary

Listen to the vocabulary words and write them down.
Go back later and fill in the correct definition for each word.

1.

2.

3.

4.

5.

6.

7.

8.

9.

10.

SHORT ANSWER UNIT TEST 2 - *Summer of My German Soldier*

I. Matching/Identify

___ 1. Anton   A. German soldier

___ 2. Sharon   B. Bergen's nanny/maid

___ 3. Edna Louise   C. Said, "God is on America's side . . ."

___ 4. Ruth   D. Hairdresser

___ 5. Harry   E. Helped Reiker

___ 6. Robert   F. Patty's pen name

___ 7. Patty   G. Patty's father

___ 8. Madlee   H. Reporter

___ 9. Freddy   I. Patty's roommate

___ 10. Reeves   J. Ruth's son

___ 11. Cauldwell   K. Boy Patty is forbidden to play with

___ 12. Mavis   L. Patty's little sister

___ 13. Antonia   M. Sheriff

Summer of My German Soldier Short Answer Unit Test 2 Page 2

II. Short Answer/Quotations - Explain the significance/importance of each of the following quotations:

1. "Christian prayers in my house!" The nerve at his temple would pulsate. Shouts of "God damn you," directed at me and maybe at Ruth. (1)

2. "Ruth did not tell me to wear this dress," I said, hating the idea of being anybody's robot. Even Ruth's. (1)

3. The secret is in absolutely refusing to let the river beat you down. If I had to, I'd measure my progress in inches. One more inch I've swum--one less inch to swim. Once you know the secret, then nobody's river can bring you down." (2)

4. "It is too. God is on America's side and anybody who's against us is on the devil's side, and that's the truth." (4)

5. "I don't feel guilty." His hand rubbed across the slight indentation in his chin. "His concern was for reward; mine was for survival." (8)

6. And now that I had of my own free will broken faith with my father and my country, I felt like a good and worthy person. (10)

Summer of My German Soldier Short Answer Unit Test 2 Page 3

7. Anton looked thoughtful. "Cruelty is after all cruelty, and the difference between the two men may have more to do with their degrees of power than their degrees of cruelty." (11)

8. "Oh, you're weak, Edna Louise," I whispered to the ring." And you're no person of value either." (14)

9. "He was good to me." (17)

10. But if Mr. Grimes calls me a prisoner, I guess he ought to know. Funny, the word has no sting. But then nothing has much sting anymore. (19)

11. "That's all they ever think about--handling me, controlling me! Why can't they just let me be?" (20)

12. "But you've got yourself some irregular seconds folks, and you've been paying more'n top dollar for them. So jest don't go a-wishing for what ain't nevah gonna be." (20)

Summer of My German Soldier Short Answer Unit Test 2 Page 4

III. Composition

    Why did Patty love Anton? Give specific examples from the novel to support your statements.

Summer of My German Soldier Short Answer Unit Test 2 Page 5

IV. Vocabulary

Listen to the vocabulary words and write them down.
Go back later and fill in the correct definition for each word.

1.

2.

3.

4.

5.

6.

7.

8.

9.

10.

KEY: SHORT ANSWER UNIT TESTS *Summer of My German Soldier*

The short answer questions are taken directly from the study guides.
If you need to look up the answers, you will find them in the study guide section.

Answers to the composition questions will vary depending on your class discussions and the level of your students.

For the vocabulary section of the test, choose ten of the words from the vocabulary lists to read orally for your students.

The answers to the matching section of the test are below.

Answers to the matching section of the Advanced Short Answer Unit Test are the same as for Short Answer Unit Test #2.

Test #1	Test #2
1. G	1. A
2. K	2. L
3. E	3. C
4. I	4. B
5. A	5. G
6. B	6. J
7. C	7. E
8. H	8. H
9. L	9. K
10. D	10. D
11. F	11. M
12. J	12. I
13. M	13. F

ADVANCED SHORT ANSWER UNIT TEST - *Summer of My German Soldier*

I. Matching

___ 1. Anton   A. German soldier

___ 2. Sharon   B. Bergen's nanny/maid

___ 3. Edna Louise   C. Said, "God is on America's side . . ."

___ 4. Ruth   D. Hairdresser

___ 5. Harry   E. Helped Reiker

___ 6. Robert   F. Patty's pen name

___ 7. Patty   G. Patty's father

___ 8. Madlee   H. Reporter

___ 9. Freddy   I. Patty's roommate

___ 10. Reeves   J. Ruth's son

___ 11. Cauldwell   K. Boy Patty is forbidden to play with

___ 12. Mavis   L. Patty's little sister

___ 13. Antonia   M. Sheriff

Summer of My German Soldier Advanced Short Answer Unit Test Page 2
II. Short Answer
1. Is the story of *Summer of My German Soldier* believable? Explain why or why not.

2. Where is the climax of the story? Explain your choice.

3. What are the main conflicts in the story and how are they resolved?

4. Describe the relationships between the following people:
    a. Patty and her father

    b. Patty and Ruth

    c. Patty and Sharon

Summer of My German Soldier Advanced Short Answer Unit Test Page 3

5. What does Patty learn during the course of the summer (by the end of the story)?

6. What can we learn from observing Patty, her family and the townspeople?

7. What does the character of Ruth add to the story?

8. Explain the role of religion in the story.

III. Composition
    Explain how *Summer of My German Soldier* is a novel against prejudice. Use as many different examples from the novel as possible to support your ideas.

Summer of My German Soldier Advanced Short Answer Unit Test Page 5

IV. Vocabulary

Write down the vocabulary words you are given. Go back later and use all of those vocabulary words in a composition relating to *Summer of My German Soldier*.

MULTIPLE CHOICE UNIT TEST 1 - *Summer of My German Soldier*

I. Matching/Identify

___ 1. Anton   A. Patty's father

___ 2. Sharon   B. Ruth's son

___ 3. Edna Louise   C. Helped Reiker

___ 4. Ruth   D. Hairdresser

___ 5. Harry   E. Said, "God is on America's side . . ."

___ 6. Robert   F. Sheriff

___ 7. Patty   G. German soldier

___ 8. Madlee   H. Reporter

___ 9. Freddy   I. Bergen's nanny/maid

___ 10. Reeves   J. Patty's roommate

___ 11. Cauldwell   K. Patty's little sister

___ 12. Mavis   L. Boy Patty is forbidden to play with

___ 13. Antonia   M. Patty's pen name

Summer of My German Soldier Multiple Choice Unit Test 1 Page 2

II. Multiple Choice

1. What does Patty's father hate?
    a. He hates the sound of children laughing and playing.
    b. He hates to see leftover food on a plate. He expects everyone to eat everything.
    c. He hates to take a favor because he doesn't like to feel obligated.
    d. He hates to hear criticisms about his merchandise.

2. Why did the P.O.W.'s come to the Bergen's store?
    a. They came to get sturdy shoes.
    b. Mr. Bergen had had prison uniforms made. They were coming to try them on.
    c. It was in the Articles of War that they could buy personal supplies.
    d. They came to buy straw field hats.

3. What was different about Reiker?
    a. He was much younger than the others.
    b. He was the only one with brown eyes.
    c. He spoke English better than the others.
    d. He was belligerent while the others seemed frightened and subdued.

4. True or False: Patty saw Anton Reiker and three of the other prisoners running toward the train. The other three got on, but Anton was not able to jump quickly enough and was left behind.
    a. True
    b. False

5. How did Anton escape from the POW camp?
    a. He dug a tunnel under the fence.
    a. He stole a delivery man's uniform and truck. His English was so good that no one suspected him.
    c. He bribed a guard by giving him fake diamonds to drive him out.
    a. He pretended to be sick and need medical attention. When the guard brought him into town to see the doctor, he ran away.

6. What was so ironic about Patty's helping Anton?
    a. Patty was the same age as his younger sister.
    b. His fiancée's name was also Patty.
    c. He had once helped a young refugee girl in Germany.
    d. Patty was Jewish.

Summer of My German Soldier Multiple Choice Unit Test 1 Page 3

7. How did Mr. Bergen and Anton react to Patty's shirt gift?
    a. They both thanked her and tried it on.
    b. Mr. Bergen said, "Thanks" and tossed it aside. Anton looked at it, felt it, and showed pleasure.
    c. Mr. Bergen yelled at her for buying from a competitor. Anton was just glad to have something to wear.
    d. Mr. Bergen ignored it. Anton liked it, but was worried that Patty would get in trouble for stealing it.

8. What comparison did Anton make?
    a. He compared Patty to a suffering saint.
    b. He compared America to heaven.
    c. He compared Mr. Bergen to Hitler.
    d. He compared himself to Patrick Henry.

9. "They are both in business to give people what they think they want." Who or what is Anton comparing?
    a. He is comparing leaders and department stores.
    b. He is comparing writers and government.
    c. He is comparing churches and salesmen.
    d. He is comparing Hitler and President Roosevelt.

10. What was Patty's plan?
    a. She would help Anton escape and then come home and act innocent.
    b. She would go with Anton.
    c. She would meet Anton in two weeks in Detroit. Then they would got to Canada.
    d. She would let him stay in the garage until the end of the war and then marry him.

11. What was Anton's last lesson for Patty?
    a. "You are a person of value and you have a friend who loved you enough to give you his most valuable possession."
    b. "Take this as a sign of my undying love. I shall return for you, no matter what it takes."
    c. "You mean more to me than life itself. You have a permanent place in my heart."
    d. "You have shown what the whole world should realize; that people of different backgrounds can indeed love and help each other."

Summer of My German Soldier Multiple Choice Unit Test 1 Page 4

12. True or False: When Harry found out about the ring, he did not believe Patty's story. He suspected that she had let a man touch her and got the gift as payment. Because of his belief, he beat her.
    a. True
    b. False

13. What happened to Anton?
    a. He successfully made it out of the country.
    b. He was captured and sent back to jail.
    c. He was shot and killed while trying to escape.
    d. He asked for and was granted political asylum in the US.

14. What was Patty's sentence?
    a. She was to spend two years on probation and live with a foster family in another town.
    b. She was to spend three months doing community service at a veteran's hospital while undergoing weekly psychiatric treatment.
    c. She was to be sent to the P.O.W. camp until the end of the war and then would be under FBI surveillance for the rest of her life.
    d. She was to spend 4 to 6 months at the Arkansas Reformatory for Girls.

15. What set Patty apart from the other girls?
    a. She was the youngest.
    b. She had a subscription to the Memphis *Commercial Appeal* newspaper.
    c. She had better clothes and had food sent in from home.
    e. Her "crime" was the most famous, and received much more publicity than any of the others.

16. To what did Patty compare Ruth's leaving?
    a. She compared it to a sunset.
    b. She compared it to having a life raft float out to sea.
    c. She compared it to a train derailing.
    d. She compared it to the birth process.

17. What did Patty learn about herself.
    a. She learned that she was a person of value who could have a happy life.
    b. She learned that she had been angry and misguided but could reform if she tried.
    c. She came to believe that there was no hope for herself.
    d. She learned that if she were mean and stubborn, she could get through any tough situation in life.

Summer of My German Soldier Multiple Choice Unit Test 1 Page 5

III. Quotations. Identify the speakers of the following quotes:
A=Patty   B=Anton   C=Grandfather   D=Mr. Bergen   E=Ruth
F=Charlene G=Edna Louise   H=Mrs. Bergen   I=Sister Parker

1. "Christian prayers in my house!" The nerve at his temple would pulsate. Shouts of "God damn you," directed at me and maybe at Ruth. (1)

2. "Ruth did not tell me to wear this dress," I said, hating the idea of being anybody's robot. Even Ruth's. (1)

3. The secret is in absolutely refusing to let the river beat you down. If I had to, I'd measure my progress in inches. One more inch I've swum--one less inch to swim. Once you know the secret, then nobody's river can bring you down." (2)

4. "It is too. God is on America's side and anybody who's against us is on the devil's side, and that's the truth." (4)

5. "I don't feel guilty." His hand rubbed across the slight indentation in his chin. "His concern was for reward; mine was for survival." (8)

6. "I don't understand. Why? How could he be so mean and then worry that he isn't loved? It doesn't make sense." (11)

7. "Cruelty is after all cruelty, and the difference between the two men may have more to do with their degrees of power than their degrees of cruelty." (11)

8. "Oh, you're weak, Edna Louise," I whispered to the ring." And you're no person of value either." (14)

9. "He was good to me." (17)

10. ". . . She's only twelve, so she didn't act wisely, O.K. But she meant good, you have to admit that." (18)

11. ". . . but do you think that if we were Protestants there would be all this hullabaloo?" (18)

12. . . . and I wondered if a blessing is still a blessing if it lasts for only a little while? (19)

13. "That's all they ever think about--handling me, controlling me! Why can't they just let me be?" (20)

Summer of My German Soldier Multiple Choice Unit Test 1 Page 6

IV. Composition

Explain how *Summer of My German Soldier* is a book about individuals loving--or not loving--other individuals. Use all the specific examples you can from the book to support your ideas.

Summer of My German Soldier Multiple Choice Unit Test 1 Page 5

IV. Vocabulary

___ 1. Relevance   a. Violation of allegiance toward one's country or cause

___ 2. Simulated   b. Chant or charm

___ 3. Incredible   c. Relevant to the matter at hand

___ 4. Pertinent   d. Beginning

___ 5. Incapable   e. Speaking of or to God in an irreverent way

___ 6. Obligated   f. Upward movement; rising spirits

___ 7. Treason   g. Lacking the ability or power

___ 8. Grotesque   h. Unbelievable

___ 9. Sarcastic   i. Widely known or recognized

___ 10. Capacity   j. The limit of ability to hold something

___ 11. Saboteurs   k. Expressive of disbelief

___ 12. Regime   l. Bizarre; having a distorted appearance

___ 13. Ascent   m. Applicability to social issues

___ 14. Incantation   n. A feeling of triumph, happiness and/or joy

___ 15. Exultation   o. Indebted; owing

___ 16. Initiating   p. Those who take treacherous action to defeat or hinder a cause

___ 17. Prominent   q. Government in power; main social structure

___ 18. Incredulous   r. Expressing cutting or ironic remarks

___ 19. Neutral   s. Not aligned with any side in a war, dispute or contest

___ 20. Blasphemy   t. Imitation

MULTIPLE CHOICE UNIT TEST 2 - *Summer of My German Soldier*

I. Matching

___ 1. Anton   A. German soldier

___ 2. Sharon   B. Bergen's nanny/maid

___ 3. Edna Louise   C. Said, "God is on America's side . . ."

___ 4. Ruth   D. Hairdresser

___ 5. Harry   E. Helped Reiker

___ 6. Robert   F. Patty's pen name

___ 7. Patty   G. Patty's father

___ 8. Madlee   H. Reporter

___ 9. Freddy   I. Patty's roommate

___ 10. Reeves   J. Ruth's son

___ 11. Cauldwell   K. Boy Patty is forbidden to play with

___ 12. Mavis   L. Patty's little sister

___ 13. Antonia   M. Sheriff

Summer of My German Soldier Multiple Choice Unit Test 2 Page 2

II. Multiple Choice

1. What does Patty's father hate?
    a. He hates the sound of children laughing and playing.
    b. He hates to see leftover food on a plate. He expects everyone to eat everything.
    c. He hates to hear criticisms about his merchandise.
    d. He hates to take a favor because he doesn't like to feel obligated.

2. Why did the P.O.W.'s come to the Bergen's store?
    a. They came to get sturdy shoes.
    b. They came to buy straw field hats.
    c. It was in the Articles of War that they could buy personal supplies.
    d. Mr. Bergen had had prison uniforms made. They were coming to try them on.

3. What was different about Reiker?
    a. He spoke English better than the others.
    b. He was the only one with brown eyes.
    c. He was much younger than the others.
    d. He was belligerent while the others seemed frightened and subdued.

4. True or False: Patty saw Anton Reiker and three of the other prisoners running toward the train. The other three got on, but Anton was not able to jump quickly enough and was left behind.
    a. True
    b. False

5. How did Anton escape from the POW camp?
    a. He dug a tunnel under the fence.
    b. He bribed a guard by giving him fake diamonds to drive him out.
    c. He stole a delivery man's uniform and truck. His English was so good that no one suspected him.
    d. He pretended to be sick and need medical attention. When the guard brought him into town to see the doctor, he ran away.

6. What was so ironic about Patty's helping Anton?
    a. Patty was Jewish.
    b. His fiancée's name was also Patty.
    c. He had once helped a young refugee girl in Germany.
    d. Patty was the same age as his younger sister.

Summer of My German Soldier Multiple Choice Unit Test 2 Page 3

7. How did Mr. Bergen and Anton react to Patty's shirt gift?
    a. They both thanked her and tried it on.
    b. Mr. Bergen yelled at her for buying from a competitor. Anton was just glad to have something to wear.
    c. Mr. Bergen said, "Thanks" and tossed it aside. Anton looked at it, felt it, and showed pleasure.
    d. Mr. Bergen ignored it. Anton liked it but was worried that Patty would get in trouble for stealing it.

8. What comparison did Anton make?
    a. He compared Patty to a suffering saint.
    b. He compared America to heaven.
    c. He compared himself to Patrick Henry.
    d. He compared Mr. Bergen to Hitler.

9. "They are both in business to give people what they think they want." Who or what is Anton comparing?"
    a. He is comparing churches and salesmen.
    b. He is comparing writers and government.
    c. He is comparing leaders and department stores.
    d. He is comparing Hitler and President Roosevelt.

10. What was Patty's plan?
    a. She would go with Anton.
    b. She would help Anton escape and then come home and act innocent.
    c. She would meet Anton in two weeks in Detroit. Then they would got to Canada.
    d. She would let him stay in the garage until the end of the war and then marry him.

11. What was Anton's last lesson for Patty?
    a. "You have shown what the whole world should realize; that people of different backgrounds can indeed love and help each other."
    b. "Take this as a sign of my undying love. I shall return for you, no matter what it takes."
    c. "You mean more to me than life itself. You have a permanent place in my heart."
    d. "You are a person of value and you have a friend who loved you enough to give you his most valuable possession."

12. True or False: When Harry found out about the ring, he believed Patty's story that a man touched her, and got the gift as payment.
    a. True
    b. False

Summer of My German Soldier Multiple Choice Unit Test 2 Page 4

13. What happened to Anton?
    a. He was shot and killed while trying to escape.
    b. He was captured and sent back to jail.
    c. He successfully made it out of the country.
    d. He asked for and was granted political asylum in the US.

14. What was Patty's sentence?
    a. She was to spend two years on probation and live with a foster family in another town.
    b. She was to spend 4 to 6 months at the Arkansas Reformatory for Girls.
    c. She was to be sent to the P.O.W. camp until the end of the war, and then would be under FBI surveillance for the rest of her life.
    a. She was to spend three months doing community service at a veteran's hospital while undergoing weekly psychiatric treatment.

15. What set Patty apart from the other girls?
    a. She was the youngest.
    a. She had better clothes and had food sent in from home.
    b. She had a subscription to the Memphis *Commercial Appeal* newspaper.
    c. Her "crime" was the most famous, and received much more publicity than any of the others.

16. To what did Patty compare Ruth's leaving?
    a. She compared it to a sunset.
    b. She compared it to the birth process.
    c. She compared it to a train derailing.
    d. She compared it to having a life raft float out to sea.

17. What did Patty learn about herself.
    a. She learned that she was a person of value who could have a happy life.
    a. She learned that she had been angry and misguided, but could reform if she tried hard enough.
    c. She came to believe that there was no hope for herself.
    d. She learned that if she were mean and stubborn, she could get through any tough situation in life.

Summer of My German Soldier Multiple Choice Unit Test 2 Page 5

III. Quotations.   Identify the speakers of the following quotes:

A=Mr. Bergen	B=Mrs. Bergen	C=Patty	D=Ruth	E=Grandfather
F=Sister Parker	G=Charlene	H=Anton	I=Edna Louise	

1. "Christian prayers in my house!" The nerve at his temple would pulsate. Shouts of "God damn you," directed at me and maybe at Ruth. (1)

2. "Ruth did not tell me to wear this dress," I said, hating the idea of being anybody's robot. Even Ruth's. (1)

3. The secret is in absolutely refusing to let the river beat you down. If I had to, I'd measure my progress in inches. One more inch I've swum--one less inch to swim. Once you know the secret, then nobody's river can bring you down." (2)

4. "It is too. God is on America's side and anybody who's against us is on the devil's side, and that's the truth." (4)

5. "I don't feel guilty." His hand rubbed across the slight indentation in his chin. "His concern was for reward; mine was for survival." (8)

6. "I don't understand. Why? How could he be so mean and then worry that he isn't loved? It doesn't make sense." (11)

7. Anton looked thoughtful. "Cruelty is after all cruelty, and the difference between the two men may have more to do with their degrees of power than their degrees of cruelty." (11)

8. "Oh, you're weak, Edna Louise," I whispered to the ring." And you're no person of value either." (14)

9. "He was good to me." (17)

10. ". . . She's only twelve, so she didn't act wisely, O.K. But she meant good, you have to admit that." (18)

11. ". . . but do you think that if we were Protestants there would be all this hullabaloo?" (18)

12. . . . and I wondered if a blessing is still a blessing if it lasts for only a little while? (19)

13. "That's all they ever think about--handling me, controlling me! Why can't they just let me be?" (20)

Summer of My German Soldier Multiple Choice Unit Test 1 Page 6

IV. Composition

Summer of My German Soldier is not only a book about looking at people as individuals instead of looking at them only as members of groups to which they may belong, it is also a book about how a young girl grows in self-confidence and learns to become an individual herself. Defend that statement using examples from the story to support your statements.

Summer of My German Soldier Multiple Choice Unit Test 2 Page 7

IV. Vocabulary

___ 1. Galvanized   a. Moving around without any particular direction

___ 2. Grotesque   b. Unbelievable

___ 3. Impassive   c. Not aligned with any side in a war, dispute or contest

___ 4. Inordinate   d. Substantial

___ 5. Formidable   e. Coated with rust-resistant zinc

___ 6. Embossed   f. Revealing no emotion

___ 7. Pertinent   g. More than is usual; extraordinary

___ 8. Tolerable   h. The limit of ability to hold something

___ 9. Milling   i. Relevant to the matter at hand

___ 10. Obligated   j. Dull

___ 11. Unaccustomed   k. Not usual; something one isn't used to

___ 12. Neutral   l. Chant or charm

___ 13. Incredible   m. Violation of allegiance toward one's country or cause

___ 14. Ascent   n. General; having no ties to a specific religion

___ 15. Capacity   o. Having a raised design

___ 16. Lackluster   p. Upward movement; rising spirits

___ 17. Treason   q. Daydream

___ 18. Incantation   r. Bearable

___ 19. Nondenominational s. Indebted; owing

___ 20. Reverie   t. Bizarre; having a distorted appearance

ANSWER SHEET - *Summer of My German Soldier*
Multiple Choice Unit Tests

I. Matching	II. Multiple Choice	III. Quotes	IV. Vocabulary
1. ___	1. ___	1. ___	1. ___
2. ___	2. ___	2. ___	2. ___
3. ___	3. ___	3. ___	3. ___
4. ___	4. ___	4. ___	4. ___
5. ___	5. ___	5. ___	5. ___
6. ___	6. ___	6. ___	6. ___
7. ___	7. ___	7. ___	7. ___
8. ___	8. ___	8. ___	8. ___
9. ___	9. ___	9. ___	9. ___
10. ___	10. ___	10. ___	10. ___
11. ___	11. ___	11. ___	11. ___
12. ___	12. ___	12. ___	12. ___
13. ___	13. ___	13. ___	13. ___
	14. ___		14. ___
	15. ___		15. ___
	16. ___		16. ___
	17. ___		17. ___
			18. ___
			19. ___
			20. ___

ANSWER KEY MULTIPLE CHOICE UNIT TESTS – *Summer of My German Soldier*

Answers to Unit Test 1 are in the left column. Answers to Unit Test 2 are in the right column.

I. Matching		II. Multiple Choice		III. Quotes		IV. Vocabulary	
1. G	A	1. C	D	1. A	C	1. M	E
2. K	L	2. D	B	2. A	C	2. T	T
3. E	C	3. C	A	3. A	C	3. H	F
4. I	B	4. B	B	4. G	I	4. C	G
5. A	G	5. C	B	5. B	H	5. G	D
6. B	J	6. D	A	6. A	C	6. O	O
7. C	E	7. B	C	7. B	H	7. A	I
8. H	H	8. C	D	8. A	C	8. L	R
9. L	K	9. A	C	9. A	C	9. R	A
10. D	D	10. B	A	10. C	E	10. J	S
11. F	M	11. A	D	11. C	E	11. P	K
12. J	I	12. A	B	12. A	C	12. Q	C
13. M	F	13. C	A	13. A	C	13. F	B
		14. D	B			14. B	P
		15. B	C			15. N	H
		16. B	D			16. D	J
		17. A	A			17. I	M
						18. K	L
						19. S	N
						20. E	Q

UNIT RESOURCE MATERIALS

BULLETIN BOARD IDEAS - *Summer of My German Soldier*

1. Save one corner of the board for the best of students' *Summer of My German Soldier* writing assignments.

2. Take one of the word search puzzles from the extra activities section and with a marker copy it over in a large size on the bulletin board. Write the clue words to find to one side. Invite students prior to and after class to find the words and circle them on the bulletin board.

3. Write several of the most significant quotations from the book onto the board on brightly colored paper.

4. Make a bulletin board listing the vocabulary words for this unit. As you complete sections of the novel and discuss the vocabulary for each section, write the definitions on the bulletin board. (If your board is one students face frequently, it will help them learn the words.)

5. Have each student bring in one picture that represents a kind of prejudice in our society. Prepare the bulletin board with background paper and a title of SUMMER OF MY GERMAN SOLDIER: A STORY AGAINST PREJUDICE. Have students post their pictures and tell what kind of prejudice their pictures represent.

6. Do a 1940's bulletin board showing dress styles, popular music, famous people of the decade, fads, etc.

7. Make a travel bulletin board about Germany--things to do and see, famous sights, places to stay, etc. (Your local travel agency can be a great source of free and low-cost materials!)

8. Do a bulletin board called GERMANY: THEN AND NOW. Make a board showing how Germany was prior to World War II, after World War II, and in the present day.

9. Make a bulletin board about careers in conjunction with the group project in Lesson Thirteen.

EXTRA ACTIVITIES

One of the difficulties in teaching a novel is that all students don't read at the same speed. One student who likes to read may take the book home and finish it in a day or two. Sometimes a few students finish the in-class assignments early. The problem, then, is finding suitable extra activities for students.

The best thing I've found is to keep a little library in the classroom. For this unit on *Summer of My German Soldier* you might check out from the school library other related books and articles about World War II, Hitler, Nazis, the Jewish religion, careers in retail businesses, military careers, careers in journalism or the media in general, prisoners of war, homeless people, or ways to help the needy.

Other things you may keep on hand are puzzles. We have made some relating directly to *Summer of My German Soldier* for you. Feel free to duplicate them.

Some students may like to draw. You might devise a contest or allow some extra-credit grade for students who draw characters or scenes from *Summer of My German Soldier*. Note, too, that if the students do not want to keep their drawings you may pick up some extra bulletin board materials this way. If you have a contest and you supply the prize (a CD or something like that perhaps), you could, possibly, make the drawing itself a non-refundable entry fee.

The pages which follow contain games, puzzles and worksheets. The keys, when appropriate, immediately follow the puzzle or worksheet. There are two main groups of activities: one group for the unit; that is, generally relating to the *Summer of My German Soldier* text, and another group of activities related strictly to the *Summer of My German Soldier* vocabulary.

Directions for these games, puzzles and worksheets are self-explanatory. The object here is to provide you with extra materials you may use in any way you choose.

MORE ACTIVITIES - *Summer of My German Soldier*

1. Pick a chapter or scene with a great deal of dialogue and have the students act it out on a stage. (Perhaps you could assign various scenes to different groups of students so more than one scene could be acted and more students could participate.)

2. Use some of the related topics noted earlier for an in-class library as topics for research, reports, or written papers, or as topics for guest speakers.

3. Have students design a book cover (front and back and inside flaps) for *Summer of My German Soldier*.

4. Have students design a bulletin board (ready to be put up; not just sketched) for *Summer of My German Soldier*.

5. Have students write a plot summary of the novel supposing that Anton had not been killed.

6. Have a 1940's day. Have students research life in the 1940s and give "show and tell" type reports and dress appropriately on your 40's day.

7. Have students rewrite the story as a diary kept by Anton, from his point of view.

8. Have your students write and tell what their "Dream Summer" would be like.

9. Explore the whole question of parents and parenting--the role and responsibility of a parent and the role and responsibility of the son or daughter. What happens to those roles in families where parents are divorced and/or remarried? What happens to those roles when teenagers have babies of their own before they have become mature adults?

10. Have an outside expert come in and talk to your class about family relationships, some common problems between parents and their children, and how those problems can be resolved.

11. Have a local news reporter come in to talk about the ethics of reporting, personal involvement in one's stories, and the responsibilities of a journalist.

12. Find out when juveniles are usually tried at your courthouse and take students there on that day to see how juveniles are treated in the justice system today.

13. Stage Patty's trial. Have students pose as prosecuting and defending attorneys, witnesses, judge, and jury.

WORD SEARCH - *Summer of My German Soldier*

All words in this list are associated with *Summer of My German Soldier*. The words are placed backwards, forward, diagonally, up and down. The included words are listed below the word searches.

```
V A L U E N E E R G R E I K E R E E V E S T A H
Z I N T L P A I L U L S E Z P N A H Q T D I Y Y
I X C B N X N Z N L T T C L J Y Y F N Q N B R Q
P R M T L G J X I F M H G Y D S M F T O D A P Q
H G R Y O M A V I S H O T G P A Y C T I N Y W S
F G V E N R S K E L H T M A Y D M N B O A O B X
C X T O G N Y M X C A A M F D J A F I D D P R T
J Y T S I U I J A P X D R E R E S T R N X B U Y
D N T K N R L P I N N B R O N Y C U I C F O O D
A C N F G M B A X A D F B E N I T W A M E K W Y
R E Y T S L C R R N W E L C D A J U D D N B Q Z
J C S R R J R G T N R R L R S A L S I G Y D X N
T M Y D Y E C P E T A G E G P D T H T D F V P X
R D M L K R Y G E H T L L P W K L R L N K V D F
L X H R C H R Q C A T Y E E J B I M A O A V W K
H S A B K E F A C I R A L R H H J G H I V T B Q
Z P A C B U H V H O L L I S S D R O W I N E Z K
```

ANTON	GREENE	MAVIS	RUTH
ANTONIA	GRIMES	NATZ	SATURDAY
APPEAL	HARRY	NAZIS	SHARON
BERGEN	HATS	PARKER	SHIRT
CAULDWELL	HIDEOUT	PATTY	SHOT
CHARLENE	HITLER	PEARL	TRAIN
DICTIONARY	HOLLIS	PIN	VALUE
EDNA	HUBCAP	RAFT	VICTORY
FBI	IRREGULAR	REEVES	WINDOW
FOOD	JENKINSVILLE	REIKER	WINE
FREDDY	LOVE	RING	WORDS
GRANDMA	MADLEE	ROBERT	

CROSSWORD - *Summer of My German Soldier*

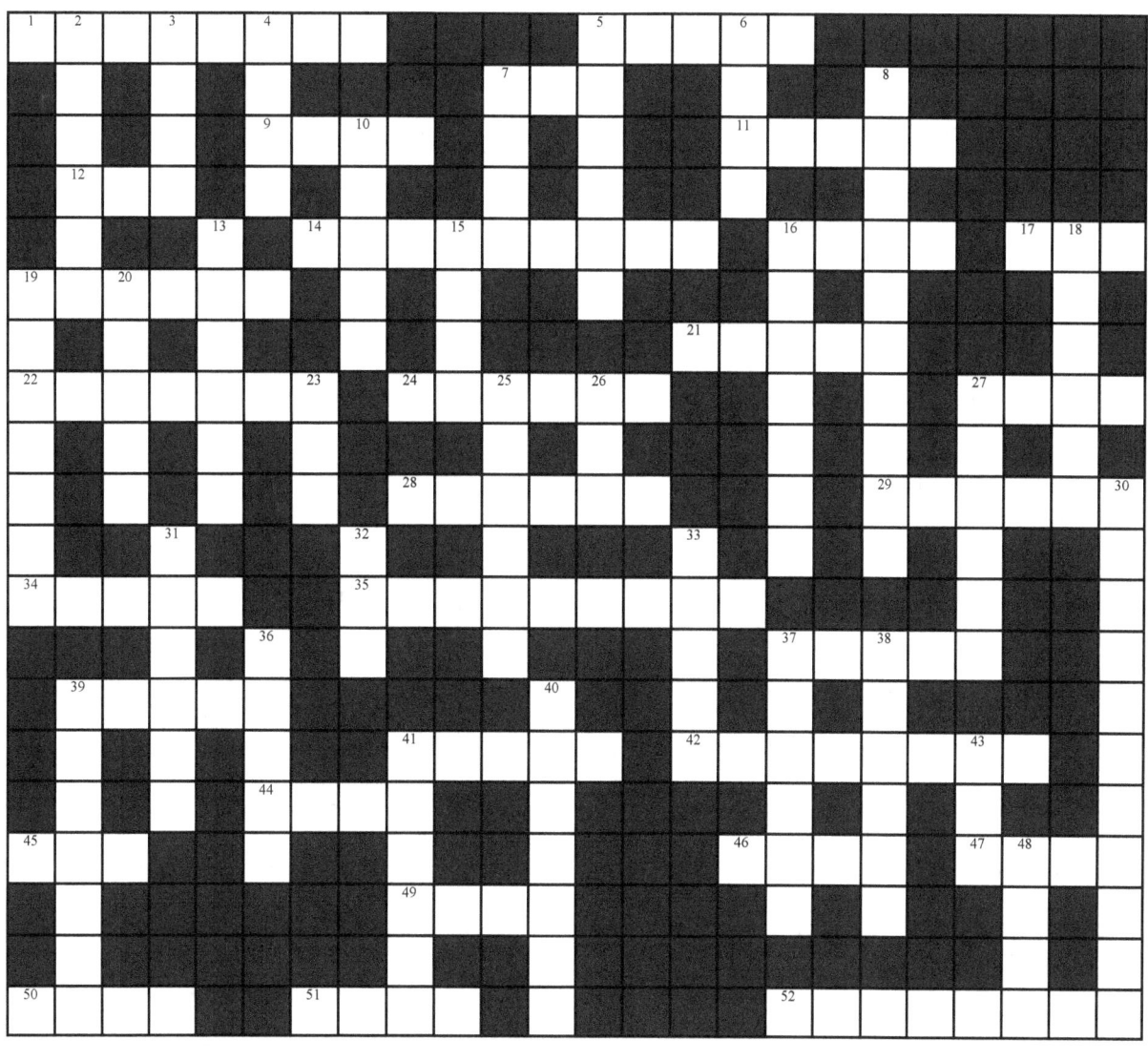

CROSSWORD CLUES - *Summer of My German Soldier*

ACROSS
1. Miss Madlee
5. Patty's father
7. They came to the store looking for information about an escapee
9. Mavis's nickname for Patty
11. They came to Jenkinsville as POWs
12. Slice
14. Sheriff
16. The POWs came to the store to buy straw ____
17. How old a person is
19. Madlee was a reporter for the Memphis Commercial _____
21. Source of war information
22. Entirely; completely
24. Patty's last name
27. Third person singular present tense of 'to go'
28. Boy Patty is forbidden to play with
29. Anton's last name
34. The German soldier
35. Ruth calls Patty's parents '_____ seconds folks'
37. Patty wants to learn the meaning of all of these
39. Anton told Patty, 'You are a person of ____....'
41. Anton looked at it, felt it, and showed pleasure at receiving this gift
42. Soldiers put them around their dugouts as protection from bullets
44. Bergen's nanny/maid
45. The German soldier --- the food
46. Belonging to you
47. Anton was ___ and killed in New York
49. It is what you do to get information from books
50. Sight organs
51. The more grown-up Patty is, the more ___ she gets in her glass
52. Patty's favorite day of the week

DOWN
2. Hit the _____; game Patty and Freddy played
3. Patty compared Ruth's leaving to this floating out to sea
4. ___ Louise; said, 'God is on America's side...'
5. Anton compared Mr. Bergen to him
6. Prized possession Anton gave Patty
7. Patty gave Anton ___ to eat
8. Patty's favorite book
10. Transportation for prisoners
13. Reporter
15. 'Nobody ____s me. In my entire life, nobody has _____ed me.'
16. Patty cleaned it from top to bottom
18. Author
19. Patty's pen name
20. Helped Reiker
23. Affirmative reply
25. Hairdresser
26. That's all; there is no more
27. He stopped for something to eat while transporting Patty
30. Arkansas _____ for Girls
31. His advice is to beware of the lawyers
32. Anton bought a gaudy one at the store
33. Patty's roommate
36. She expected her father to give Harry a job
37. A car one got broken
38. Ruth's son
39. Kind of garden people were supposed to have
40. It was okay for Sharon to take money from her
41. Patty's sister
43. Fuel for tanks, trucks, cars, etc.
48. Difficult

CROSSWORD - *Summer of My German Soldier*

MATCHING QUIZ/WORKSHEET 1 - *Summer of My German Soldier*

___ 1. PARKER

___ 2. SHOT

___ 3. CAULDWELL

___ 4. MAVIS

___ 5. MADLEE

___ 6. SUBSCRIPTION

___ 7. VALUE

___ 8. NAZIS

___ 9. WORDS

___ 10. HIDEOUT

___ 11. IRREGULAR

___ 12. GRANDMA

___ 13. REIKER

___ 14. WINDOW

___ 15. REFORMATORY

___ 16. NATZ

___ 17. GREENE

___ 18. HATS

___ 19. SATURDAY

___ 20. SHIRT

A. Anton looked at it, felt it, and showed pleasure at receiving this gift

B. They came to Jenkinsville as POWs

C. Author

D. Ruth calls Patty's parents '_____ seconds folks'

E. Anton was ___ and killed in New York

F. The POWs came to the store to buy straw ____

G. It was okay for Sharon to take money from her

H. Patty lied to Sister ___, saying Anton hated Hitler

I. Mavis's nickname for Patty

J. Anton told Patty, 'You are a person of ___....'

K. Patty's roommate

L. Miss Madlee gave one to Patty

M. A car one got broken

N. Reporter

O. Patty cleaned it from top to bottom

P. Arkansas _____ for Girls

Q. Patty's favorite day of the week

R. Patty wants to learn the meaning of all of these

S. Sheriff

T. Anton's last name

MATCHING QUIZ/WORKSHEET 2 - *Summer of My German Soldier*

___ 1. PATTY   A. Patty's favorite book

___ 2. EDNA   B. Patty's last name

___ 3. VICTORY   C. Boy Patty is forbidden to play with

___ 4. PIN   D. Anton bought a gaudy one at the store

___ 5. DICTIONARY   E. Mavis's nickname for Patty

___ 6. SHIRT   F. Anton's last name

___ 7. HATS   G. Anton told Patty, 'You are a person of ___....'

___ 8. MAVIS   H. Kind of garden people were supposed to have

___ 9. REEVES   I. Hit the _____; game Patty and Freddy played

___ 10. VALUE   J. Patty cleaned it from top to bottom

___ 11. FBI   K. ___ Louise; said, 'God is on America's side...'

___ 12. HUBCAP   L. Patty's roommate

___ 13. NATZ   M. Helped Reiker

___ 14. HIDEOUT   N. They came to the store looking for information about an escapee

___ 15. ROBERT   O. Patty gave Anton ___ to eat

___ 16. FOOD   P. Anton looked at it, felt it, and showed pleasure at receiving this gift

___ 17. GREENE   Q. The POWs came to the store to buy straw ____.

___ 18. BERGEN   R. Author

___ 19. FREDDY   S. Hairdresser

___ 20. REIKER   T. Ruth's son

KEY: MATCHING QUIZ/WORKSHEETS - *Summer of My German Soldier*

Worksheet 1	Worksheet 2
1. H	1. M
2. E	2. K
3. S	3. H
4. K	4. D
5. N	5. A
6. L	6. P
7. J	7. Q
8. B	8. L
9. R	9. S
10. O	10. G
11. D	11. N
12. G	12. I
13. T	13. E
14. M	14. J
15. P	15. T
16. I	16. O
17. C	17. R
18. F	18. B
19. Q	19. C
20. A	20. F

JUGGLE LETTER REVIEW GAME CLUE SHEET - *Summer of My German Soldier*

SCRAMBLED	WORD	CLUE
ELPPAA	APPEAL	Madlee was a reporter for the Memphis *Commercial* _____
ODEHUTI	HIDEHOUT	Patty cleaned it from top to bottom
APYTT	PATTY	Helped Reiker
DSWRO	WORDS	Patty wants to learn the meaning of all of these
NEWI	WINE	The more grown up Patty is, the more _____ she gets in her glass
EHLRIT	HITLER	Anton compared Mr. Bergen to him
RUIAELRRG	IRREGULAR	Ruth calls Patty's parents _____ seconds folks
AVISM	MAVIS	Patty's roommate
NOAAITN	ANTONIA	Patty's pen name
RSTHI	SHIRT	Anton looked at it, felt it, and showed pleasure at receiving this gift
ELVAU	VALUE	Anton told Patty, "'You are a person of ____"
BERRTO	ROBERT	Ruth's son
DOFO	FOOD	Patty gave Anton _____ to eat
LEADME	MADLEE	Reporter
OVEL	LOVE	'Nobody _____'s me. In my entire life, nobody has _____ed me.'
IFB	FBI	They came to the store looking for information about an escapee
BHPUCA	HUBCAP	Hit the _____; game Patty and Freddy played
LLIOSH	HOLLIS	His advice is to beware of the lawyers
NTOAN	ANTON	The German soldier
NAROSH	SHARON	Patty's sister
UCPIBNSRSTIO	SUBSCRIPTION	Miss Madlee gave one to Patty
ERPLA	PEARL	She expected her father to give Harry a job
TZAN	NATZ	Mavis's nickname for Patty
TTYAP	PATTY	Helped Reiker
CRIAONYITD	DICTIONARY	Patty's favorite book
NIRTA	TRAIN	Transportation for prisoners
AINSZ	NAZIS	They came to Jenkinsville as POWs
TSAH	HATS	The POWs came to the store to buy straw _____
RYDDEF	FREDDY	Boy Patty is forbidden to play with
ENRHCLEA	CHARLENE	Miss Madlee
AKEPRR	PARKER	Patty lied to Sister _____, saying Anton hated Hitler

TRHSI	SHIRT	Anton looked at it, felt it, and showed pleasure at receiving this gift
NRBEGE	BERGEN	Patty's last name
ARYHR	HARRY	Patty's father
NGIR	RING	Prized possession Anton gave Patty
YTVOCIR	VICTORY	Kind of garden people were supposed to have
ESEERV	REEVES	Hairdresser
HTRU	RUTH	Bergen's nanny/maid

VOCABULARY RESOURCE MATERIALS

VOCABULARY WORD SEARCH - *Summer of My German Soldier*

All words in this list are associated with *Summer of My German Soldier* with an emphasis on the vocabulary words chosen for study in the text. The words are placed backwards, forward, diagonally, up and down. The included words are listed below.

```
I N C R E D I B L E U N A C C U S T O M E D E Q
X N Z L C T L F O S R N I T W K O V F J W I W D
B T T N D X A B E M S T O K N L F F D C R R J L
C R H A V B L S Q E S K S S E M Y N N E W K J S
C A P A C I T Y L A B K D R A M M I V N X T Y P
Z P V R G T P Y C U G L A I E E N E O T E J M X
N T J A T R Q R K W P B E H N I R I J L G S N E
H M T C Q Y A Y D C L E P K T C T T B X I O V R
D E M B O S S E D E C S Q I V C A A B N I I B B
D R Y T H Z T L V N A L A L I C D P O T S B L Y
R X E V N A Q C A L L T A V Z I T R A S F E N B
P F F S L W R V B D I Z N R M N D T A B A P L T
P C C U O H E E G N S O J R T I L P D K L W N Z
Q G M I L L I N G D C S O F N U M I N G L E D X
T I W T E D U R Z I I F K A X I E E Z F C P Y P
S M S R N N S T Z P M R T E X G S N W S J H B M
C T N E N I T R E P Z E E P P S L T A N H T N F
```

ASCENT	FEEBLE	MILLING	RESOLUTE
BLASPHEMY	FORMIDABLE	MINGLED	REVERIE
BLEAKNESS	IMPASSIVE	NEUTRAL	SARCASTIC
CAPACITY	INCAPABLE	OBLIGATED	SIMULATED
CONVICTION	INCREDIBLE	PERTINENT	TOLERABLE
DIRE	INITIATING	PULSATE	TREASON
EMBOSSED	INORDINATE	REGIME	UNACCUSTOMED
EXULTATION	INTACT	RELEVANCE	

VOCABULARY CROSSWORD - *Summer of My German Soldier*

VOCABULARY CROSSWORD CLUES - *Summer of My German Soldier*

ACROSS

1. Characteristic of being convincing or believable
4. Moving around without any particular direction
8. Fatigue
13. Indebted; owing
15. Wager
16. Patty compared Ruth's leaving to this floating out to sea
17. Sight organs
18. Remaining whole or uninjured
19. Speaking of or to God in an irreverent way
22. Opposite of buy
24. Twisted out of shape
26. Anton would -- the food Patty brought
27. Give free of charge
28. Unusual
29. They came to the store looking for information about an escapee
31. Weak
34. Patty's sister
35. Expand and contract rhythmically; beat
37. Those who take treacherous action to defeat or hinder a cause
40. A car one got broken
41. Anton looked at it, felt it, and showed pleasure at receiving this gift
43. His advice is to beware of the lawyers
44. ___ Louise; said, 'God is on America's side...'
45. Hazy; indefinite; not precise
46. The repetition of the same sounds at the beginning of words

DOWN

2. Not aligned with any side in a war, dispute or contest
3. Also
4. Mixed
5. 'Nobody ____s me. In my entire life, nobody has _____ed me.'
6. Coated with rust-resistant zinc
7. A feeling of triumph, happiness and/or joy
8. Having a raised design
9. The POWs came to the store to buy straw ____
10. General; having no ties to a specific religion
11. Cunningly
12. The limit of ability to hold something
14. Violation of allegiance toward one's country or cause
19. Gloominess; dreariness
20. Upward movement; rising spirits
21. Anton bought a gaudy one at the store
23. Bizarre; having a distorted appearance
25. Urgent; desperate; having terrible consequences
30. Revealing no emotion
31. Possessed with or motivated by excessive zeal
32. Patty gave Anton ___ to eat
33. Government in power; main social structure
36. Patty wants to learn the meaning of all of these
38. Anton was ___ and killed in New York
39. Prized possession Anton gave Patty
42. The more grown-up Patty is, the more ___ she gets in her glass

VOCABULARY CROSSWORD - *Summer of My German Soldier*

VOCABULARY WORKSHEET 1 - *Summer of My German Soldier*

___ 1. REPROACHFULLY   A. Gloominess; dreariness

___ 2. FANATICAL   B. Imitation

___ 3. FEEBLE   C. A feeling of triumph, happiness and/or joy

___ 4. BLASPHEMY   D. Expressing blame or a reprimand

___ 5. NONDENOMINATIONAL   E. Weak

___ 6. INCANTATION   F. Fatigue

___ 7. NEUTRAL   G. Mixed

___ 8. INORDINATE   H. Twisted out of shape

___ 9. FORMIDABLE   I. Daydream

___ 10. MINGLED   J. Widely known or recognized

___ 11. REVERIE   K. Speaking of or to God in an irreverent way

___ 12. BLEAKNESS   L. Lacking the ability or power

___ 13. EMBOSSED   M. Having a raised design

___ 14. INCAPABLE   N. Substantial

___ 15. EXHAUSTION   O. More than is usual; extraordinary

___ 16. PROMINENT   P. Chant or charm

___ 17. CONTORTED   Q. Possessed with or motivated by excessive zeal

___ 18. EXULTATION   R. The limit of ability to hold something

___ 19. CAPACITY   S. Not aligned with any side in a war, dispute or contest

___ 20. SIMULATED   T. General; having no ties to a specific religion

VOCABULARY WORKSHEET 2 - *Summer of My German Soldier*

___ 1. Beginning
    a. Presumptuous   b. Initiating   c. Contorted   d. Pertinent

___ 2. Indebted; owing
    a. Incredulous   b. Initiating   c. Obligated   d. Impassive

___ 3. Expressing cutting or ironic remarks
    a. Palatable   b. Saboteurs   c. Resolute   d. Sarcastic

___ 4. A feeling of triumph, happiness and/or joy
    a. Exultation   b. Reproachfully   c. Contorted   d. Nondenominational

___ 5. Remaining whole or uninjured
    a. Intact   b. Obligated   c. Lackluster   d. Tolerable

___ 6. Violation of allegiance toward one's country or cause
    a. Prominent   b. Treason   c. Initiating   d. Neutral

___ 7. Having a raised design
    a. Embossed   b. Initiating   c. Exultation   d. Lackluster

___ 8. Moving around without any particular direction
    a. Reverie   b. Galvanized   c. Neutral   d. Milling

___ 9. Bizarre; having a distorted appearance
    a. Tolerable   b. Grotesque   c. Prominent   d. Fanatical

___ 10. Dull
    a. Relevance   b. Reverie   c. Intact   d. Lackluster

___ 11. Widely known or recognized
    a. Feeble   b. Prominent   c. Relevance   d. Sarcastic

___ 12. Substantial
    a. Formidable   b. Simulated   c. Neutral   d. Pertinent

___ 13. The limit of ability to hold something
    a. Galvanized   b. Unaccustomed   c. Capacity   d. Mingled

___ 14. Upward movement; rising spirits
    a. Lackluster   b. Ascent   c. Formidable   d. Contorted

___ 15. Imitation
    a. Formidable   b. Pertinent   c. Simulated   d. Intact

___ 16. Those who take treacherous action to defeat or hinder a cause
    a. Regime   b. Conviction   c. Saboteurs   d. Impassive

___ 17. Possessed with or motivated by excessive zeal
    a. Incredulous   b. Presumptuous   c. Fanatical   d. Neutral

___ 18. Expressing blame or a reprimand
    a. Fanatical   b. Formidable   c. Reproachfully   d. Reverie

___ 19. Chant or charm
    a. Conviction   b. Incantation   c. Neutral   d. Inordinate

___ 20. Expressive of disbelief
    a. Tolerable   b. Incredulous   c. Reverie   d. Presumptuous

KEY: VOCABULARY WORKSHEETS - *Summer of My German Soldier*

Worksheet 1	Worksheet 2
1. D	1. B
2. Q	2. C
3. E	3. D
4. K	4. A
5. T	5. A
6. P	6. B
7. S	7. A
8. O	8. D
9. N	9. B
10. G	10. D
11. I	11. B
12. A	12. A
13. M	13. C
14. L	14. A
15. F	15. C
16. J	16. C
17. H	17. C
18. C	18. C
19. R	19. B
20. B	20. B

VOCABULARY JUGGLE LETTER REVIEW GAME CLUES
Summer of My German Soldier

SCRAMBLED	WORD	CLUE
ODEUILUNSCR	INCREDULOUS	Expressive of disbelief
LRNAUTE	NEUTRAL	Not aligned with any side in a war, dispute or contest
TOUPESMRSUUP	PRESUMPTUOUS	Excessively forward
NAMOUDCSTECU	UNACCUSTOMED	Not usual; something one isn't used to
TERSOBSUA	SABOTEURS	Those who take treacherous action to defeat or hinder a cause
TNESAC	ASCENT	Upward movement; rising spirits
ALVEGIANDZ	GALVANIZED	Coated with rust-resistant zinc
TAULEPS	PULSATE	Expand and contract rhythmically; beat
EBEFEL	FEEBLE	Weak
SBKELEANS	BLEAKNESS	Gloominess; dreariness
REIPNNTMO	PROMINENT	Widely known or recognized
ARELLBEOT	TOLERABLE	Bearable
NDECRILEIB	INCREDIBLE	Unbelievable
TABEDOIGL	OBLIGATED	Indebted; owing
AEILCBNAP	INCAPABLE	Lacking the ability or power
ATLACANIF	FANATICAL	Possessed with or motivated by excessive zeal
CRTSSICAA	SARCASTIC	Expressing cutting or ironic remarks
IEDR	DIRE	Urgent; desperate; having terrible consequences
TUDIAESML	SIMULATED	Imitation
NILMGIL	MILLING	Moving around without any particular direction
LBDIMRFEOA	FORMIDABLE	Substantial
LEENAVERC	RELEVANCE	Applicability to social issues
LDEIMGN	MINGLED	Moving around without any particular direction
HRFCLOUPYEARL	REPROACHFULLY	Expressing blame or a reprimand
TSRQEEUOG	GROTESQUE	Bizarre; having a distorted appearance
TDORNCETO	CONTORTED	Twisted out of shape
TUOISNEAHX	EXHAUSTION	Fatigue
IPAACTYC	CAPACITY	The limit of ability to hold something
ENOTRSA	TREASON	Violation of allegiance toward one's country or cause
LTTOUINAXE	EXULTATION	A feeling of triumph, happiness and/or joy

ORTAENDNII	INORDINATE	More than is usual, extraordinary
ITPNEENRT	PERTINENT	Relevant to the matter at hand
EGMERI	REGIME	Government in power; main social structure
ERIREVE	REVERIE	Daydream
MDEBEOSS	EMBOSSED	Having a raised design
LUORTESE	RESOLUTE	Expressing firm determination
IIANIINTGT	INITIATING	Beginning
ATNTIC	INTACT	Remaining whole or uninjured
IVTONICCNO	CONVICTION	Characteristic of being convincing or believable

www.ingramcontent.com/pod-product-compliance
Lightning Source LLC
Chambersburg PA
CBHW051414070526
44584CB00023B/3429